Reveal. Love. Manifest.

A 63 Day Guide to Manifesting Your Goals Through Self Discovery and the Power of Affirmations.

Victoria Dumé

D1067133

CONTENTS

REVEAL. LOVE. MANIFEST.

INTRODUCTION

Welcome to the next 63 days of your life. This 63 day workbook and guide is created to align you with your goals through a self discovery method I like to call "Reveal to Heal." Along with daily affirmations this guide will help rewire your old ways of thinking that have kept you from achieving your goals. These affirmations will help you release limiting beliefs, and stories that have been holding you back from fully stepping into a new way of being. This guided affirmation workbook will also help shift your pattern of thinking and acting from a lack and limited mindset to a mindset of abundance and gratitude. I chose 63 days because there is a popular belief by many that it takes 21 days to create new habits and change old habits. And some say that it takes 3 cycles of 21 days for those new habits to fully take on. So I have decided to create this guide and workbook into 3 parts. Each part is 21 days long.

Here is what you can look forward to accomplishing on this 63 day journey:

The first 21 days is your Reveal to Heal journey. In the first 21 days you will become aware of the patterns of thoughts and the stories that have kept you in a lack mindset. As I always love to say, "you must check yourself before you wreck yourself." Here you will find out the reasons why you are not achieving your ultimate goals and desires. You will begin to see how you can start to shift your thoughts and patterns of thinking to create more abundance and happiness in your life. You will discover whether your thoughts and words are either aligning you to your goals or distancing you and blocking you from achieving those goals.

The second 21 days is your journey of Self Love and Forgiveness. Discover truly what it means to have self love and how forgiveness is not just for you to give to others but for you to receive as well. It is here where you get to a place where you truly lack nothing. You will discover you are whole and complete and a perfect creation. It's time to "Let it Go!" Let go of any and all external attachments for fulfillment, love, and validation. Free yourself from self loathing and the damage that self loathing communication has on your mind, body, and your overall health. If you are functioning in a mindset rooted in self loathing, shame, and guilt, you are not able to give your mind and body the fuel and energy it needs to thrive. During these 21 days you will see that unless your energy and spirit is rooted in and fueled by love and gratitude, you are depriving yourself of the highest energetic fuel to achieve and manifest your ultimate desires.

The last 21 days of your 63 day journey is where the magic begins. Here is where you will write and create your affirmations as your full authentic self. Your new abundant mindset has taken hold. You have discovered the old patterns and ways of thinking and being that have kept you in bondage and lack, and you are now stepping into a new way of being. You are creating a reality where new possibilities exist. Nothing from your past is here. You are now stepping into your highest self and the best version of yourself. You get to create your future through the power of gratitude and the power of affirmations. Here you are in alignment with the promises of God and the greatness you were created for. No more hiding, no more limits, no boundaries.

Each of the 21 days will have its own unique affirmation that I have written for you. However, I suggest that you create your own set of affirmations for each of the 21 days. I have written for you on page 131 a set of affirmations that you can pull from to write out your own affirmation statement. Feel free to use any of those. The important part is that you will write and read the same affirmation for those 21 days.
So, as you go into the next 21 days you will have a new affirmation statement pertaining to the area we are working through. It is important that you have the same affirmation throughout those 21 days because repetition is essential to memorizing and programming your beliefs. As you will discover throughout these next 63 days, we have limiting beliefs from our past that have taken over and have blocked us from achieving our goals. Because of this, creating and reprogramming those old beliefs is essential to our transformation.

Let's also start by understanding that the personal development and growth journey is multi level. Unraveling and discovering the deep-rooted subconscious beliefs and thoughts that are in control of your life is where it begins. There are many levels of personal growth, and for most people they only begin to scratch the surface of what true personal development is. But again there are levels within levels of personal development. It's a constant journey of discovery and growth, and the deeper you are willing to go the more growth and transformation you will acquire. We don't just stop at what I like to call your 2.0 version, we keep upgrading to 3.0 and beyond. It's going to take conscious effort to overcome the subconscious battle.

Personal development is not just about creating worldly success, it's about creating true personal joy and happiness to the core of your being. This happiness is found inside of you because God created you perfect and whole from day 1. It was only when you allowed the world and the consequences of limiting beliefs to tell you otherwise, that you began to forget that you already possess the power to be complete, whole, and abundantly prosperous. The Bible in John 10:10 reminds us that we are called to have life abundantly, full and a satisfying life, and it reminds us that the thief comes only to steal and destroy. How may have you fallen prey to the schemes of the world? Who has stolen your joy? Has the thief robbed you from believing that your desires and a prosperous life are not yours to have? In order to get to the core of your being we have to start really unraveling the layers that have begun to callus you, harden you, and lead you astray.

If you are willing to start the unraveling process and begin to reveal what has been taking the driver's seat of your life, then you can truly begin to heal. Each day there will be journaling prompts that are part of this discovery process. Journaling your thoughts and asking yourself the deep questions is essential to transformation. There is no right or wrong answer, so do not overthink the answers. Focus on releasing the emotions and allow yourself to free up the thoughts that are consuming you. Journaling will allow you to start taking control of your thoughts and emotions and will also reveal your triggers. You will be able to start marking connections about your emotions, behaviors, thoughts, and deeply rooted beliefs. Most importantly, journaling can change your life. So let's start to Reveal and Heal.

Part 1: Reveal

DAY 1: IT STARTS WITH GRATITUDE

If you are anything like I was about 3 years ago, I very much thought I was living a life of gratitude. But I quickly realized that was not so. You see, just like personal development is layers deep, so are the concepts, lifestyle practices, modalities, and strategies within personal development. Three years ago, I realized that my concept and idea of gratitude was a very surface level comprehension of gratitude. Once I discovered what it really meant to live a life fueled by and rooted in gratitude, I was awake to the very reasons why my life seemed to be creating more lack than abundance. There's a very good chance that you too are in the same boat. Don't worry. I will explain more each day why this is so.

Awareness will always be key to a life of transformation. Having a deeper level of awareness will allow you to make the changes necessary at a conscious level to shift you into a life of abundance.

Here is my discovery of what a life fueled by gratitude means. A life fueled by gratitude means a life where you see growth and abundance versus lack and limitations. Gratitude allows you to be free to surrender control to a higher power. Gratitude doesn't live in lack, fear, or worry, because it is optimistic and thrives in faith and hopes for the best. A life fueled in gratitude expects and prepares for the best case scenarios versus the worst case scenarios. It doesn't align with self-doubt, self-loathing, or a victim mindset. Instead, it has love and understanding, and sees opportunities everywhere.

A life fueled by gratitude doesn't compare or allow jealousy to infiltrate your mind. You are victorious. A super conqueror. You are never a victim. You believe that all things work out, because you step into a place of faith and love. You surrender to a higher power who orchestrates it all, because you are in alignment with all that is good, perfect, and complete. You lack nothing. You are aware of the promises of God and his universal laws, and your actions and ways of being are in discernment with those very promises. You are in alignment with love, healing, forgiveness, and abundance.

Gratitude shifts your way of seeing things. It sees challenges and difficulties as opportunities and lessons. It creates growth and strength from resistance. You will begin to see all your triggers as revelations of where you might be lacking freedom, and through unraveling and discovery, you will now be able to grow and step into a place of true freedom.

Gratitude doesn't allow you to dwell in a place of lack, pain, and low emotional energy. Rather, gratitude allows you to feel the full spectrum of your emotions and then reset. You feel calmer and more patient. Your self confidence increases and you start to trust yourself. Your intuition is stronger and you start seeing more possibilities rather than problems. You are more loving and giving, because you now know there is nothing you lack, and that you are surrounded by abundance.

Daily Journal Prompt:

1. What areas of your life have you lacked gratitude in?
2. List 10 things you are grateful for.

Affirmation: I allow myself to let go of beliefs that were never mine. I accept myself for who I am with all the experiences I have had and I am ready to step into my true potential.

DAY 2: IT'S ALL ABOUT YOUR MINDSET

Before I started to really dig deeper into my personal development journey and really start this unraveling process, I was not aware that there were different mindsets and ways of thinking about life that dominated our ways of being. As we enter into day 2, I would like to spend some time discussing what is known as a "Lack Mindset."

A lack mindset is rooted in scarcity. In this mindset you will always find evidence of scarcity all around. A lack mindset says that there is not enough for everyone, that only some are lucky enough to create abundance, and that some are more favored than others.

This lack mindset will affect the way you see money, love, and opportunities. A lack mindset is pessimistic and rarely can see success in most situations and opportunities. In this mindset you tend to see what is going wrong and what could go wrong versus what is right and what could go right. A lack mindset is also rooted in fear versus faith. It causes limitations, and imposes a threat of never having enough money, time, rest, health, or love. Living in a lack mindset will limit your desires, limit the risks you take in life, and limit your ability to truly leap with faith to chase your dreams. A lack mindset (also known as scarcity consciousness) could be the very reasons why your day to day actions and experiences are not allowing you to step into a life fueled by gratitude. Let's discover how a lack mindset might be affecting you.

Daily Journal Prompt:

1. Do you often find yourself fearful, anxious, and worried about the future?
2. Do you applaud and celebrate when others are successful and winning, or does it make you judgmental, or jealous of their success?
3. Do you feel you must compete with others for jobs, relationships, and money, or do you have faith that you will always have what you need?
4. Do you compare yourself to others?
5. Are you quick to see the problems vs the solutions?
6. Do you doubt your ability to succeed? If you are successful in your work, do you feel the pressure to be more, make more money, and have more than you do right now?

Affirmation: I allow myself to let go of beliefs that were never mine. I accept myself for who I am with all the experiences I have had. I am ready to step into my true potential.

DAY 3: ARE YOU AUTHENTIC?

As we continue to unravel the parts of your life that have kept you from stepping into who you truly were created to be, there is a version of you inside that knows your worth, your value, your power, and your amazing potential. Over time events, circumstances, relationships, and experiences begin to tell you otherwise. The world begins to steal your true identity, and you subtly begin to unknowingly conform and take on a little bit more of the world as your identity. Sooner or later you are fully dressed in a wardrobe that was picked out by others rather than yourself. But there is a version of you that is real and authentic, and desires badly to emerge. My goal is to help you release that powerful version of yourself.

Many of us have taken on identities not just about our personality, but about our potential and our abilities as well. You might find yourself believing that you are not talented or smart enough. Maybe it's that you are not lucky like others. Do you ever feel you are not as favored or liked as much as others are? Do you find yourself wanting to be liked by everyone? What is your belief about your ability to create wealth and abundance? Does money come easily to you? Is money evil? Does money cause problems? Do you want more money, but seem to find it difficult to have more of it or keep it? Is love available for you? Do you believe love is hard or that love hurts? Are there no good partners out there? Do you find conflict between your desires and the belief you have the ability to achieve them? Is your health in alignment with what you want? Is health and diet difficult for you? Do you believe you have or don't have good genes that promote good health? Why do you believe that? Think about these concepts and break down your personal goals and desires. Think deeply on the stories, ideas, and identities you have attached to your way of being and believing that don't feel right, or that come in between what you desire and what you believe you can have. Unravel those beliefs and think about why you believe them. Think about what events or situations have created this way of believing for you. In the personal development world, we call these agreements. Agreements are beliefs that are deeply rooted in your mind as truths. From the time we were very young, these agreements have been put on us by our family, society, religion, and other organizations. These agreements feed our fears and doubts. But when we navigate through those fears and doubts, we can actually find where we truly desire to go. To do so, you must start letting go of what you think you know.

Daily Journal Prompt:

1. What parts of your life are you aware are inauthentic?
2. What holds you back from doing more of the things you love to do?
3. What areas of life do you want to explore more of?
4. What skills and talents do you want to increase?
5. What beliefs about money, love, health, and opportunities do you want to be true for you?

Affirmation: I allow myself to let go of beliefs that were never mine. I accept myself for who I am with all the experiences I have had. I am ready to step into my true potential.

DAY 4: WIRED TO SURVIVE

You are wired for survival and you are also programmed for comfort. If you are not careful, you will get "way too comfortable" in the comfort zone and settle for a life not meant for you. Even when your "comfort zone" is unhealthy, harmful, and painful, you could find yourself retreating back to that comfort zone if you're not aware of your deep subconscious beliefs that have you sabotaging your own goals and desires. Unless you are consciously aware of this survival mode, you will always revert to the level of comfort you've been programmed to accept. Even when a new reality emerges that is much better than the one you have been comfortable in, you could find yourself right back to where you started if you don't create a new mindset and belief. This is why you will see many women jump from unhealthy relationships to another unhealthy relationship. This is why you will see people who are poor and no matter how much money they earn or win, they will remain broke. And... this is why you will see overweight people who lose weight but then revert back to being overweight rather than maintaining their weight off. As we discussed on day 3, there is an identity you have taken on over time, and that identity has a story attached to it. If that story says "I'm unworthy, I'm not smart, I'm broke, I'm fat," and so on, then that identity is what you will unconsciously navigate right back to.

Let's reveal what identity and story you have created about yourself. Let's become aware of the parts of this identity and story that are either holding you back, or moving you forward. Question number one is about all the ways you have created an identity about who you are. For example: "I'm always late, I am such a messy person, I am neatfreak, I am fat, I am a hot mess, I am so forgetful, I am shy, I am loud, I am clumsy, I am not good at cooking." Write down the "I am" statements that you have taken on as your identity.

Daily Journal Prompt:

1. Write as many "I am" statements about yourself as possible:
2. How are these "I am" statements in conflict with your goals and desires?
3. What stories about your life have you created about who you are that are keeping you from accomplishing your goals and dreams?
4. Write down 10 new "I am" statements that will be your new future identity. As you journey on in this book, you will affirm and align yourself with this new identity. Feel free to use some of the affirmations from page 126

Affirmation: I allow myself to let go of beliefs that were never mine. I accept myself for who I am with all the experiences I have had. I am ready to step into my true potential.

DAY 5: THE COCOON

To begin any real actions of change and growth you must first become aware of yourself. So we continue on revealing and unraveling. Transformation is not always easy and fun. Taking on some parts of this 63 day process is going to feel uncomfortable and may even feel defeating. But your desire and willingness to change the way you have been programmed to think (even change the automatic instinctual ways you react) will start to rewire your perception of yourself and redefine the possibilities in front of you. This is the exciting part! This will keep you from reverting back to old patterns that were holding you back. I love to use the example of the caterpillar transforming into the butterfly. In order to arrive at its new form, it has to first become entombed in its cocoon and metamorphosize. This is the most painful and toughest thing it will encounter.

Without knowing it, you are automatically creating knowable outcomes to reaffirm your beliefs as you "know" them to be. You will always find evidence for those beliefs. Being attached to those beliefs doesn't allow for any other new possibility because your world view is filtered through those beliefs. Those thoughts and beliefs are either empowering you or disempowering you.

All your senses will also confirm this reality because your brain is filtering all the sensory input that you are feeding it through those same beliefs. What you smell, see, taste, feel, and hear all serve to reaffirm those deeply held beliefs.

And, because your senses are attached to those beliefs, the inputs remain the same, and you keep creating the same experiences.

If you are always thinking the same way and reacting the same way, then you will always create the same way. So... how can you ever change anything?

Let's reveal some areas of your life that you feel always remain the same or always revert back to the way they were.

Daily Journal Prompt:

1. Write down the parts of your life, health, money, love, friendships, and/or careers that always remain the same or are inconsistent.
2. What stories have you attached to those parts of your life?

Affirmation: I allow myself to let go of beliefs that were never mine. I accept myself for who I am with all the experiences I have had. I am ready to step into my true potential.

DAY 6: LEAVE THE PAST BEHIND

You have seen that past beliefs and experiences and failures have shifted your perceptions about life and what you are truly capable of achieving. Maybe you have some strong desires and goals but you keep hitting a wall, or you find yourself giving up on those goals or delaying the actions you need to take. Could it be that the reason you delay or hit those walls is because you have a story attached to it? What are your thoughts? Do they say it's too hard? Do they say you're not good enough or smart enough? Maybe you fear what you may lose if you truly go after your goals?

Maybe now you are aware that there are areas of your life you are not leaping into with faith. Instead you may be taking the path of least resistance. Maybe you are finding yourself running towards comfort and convenience rather than taking the big actions needed to achieve your goals. I don't believe God created you for comfort and mediocrity. I believe he created you for greatness and for living a life of full power and freedom.

Daily Journal Prompt:

1. Write a powerful statement today outlining the steps you desire to take moving forward that will be in alignment with your goals.
2. What stories and past identity will you need to let go of in order to step into these actions?

Affirmation:I allow myself to let go of beliefs that were never mine. I accept myself for who I am with all the experiences I have had. I am ready to step into my true potential.

DAY 7: LET IT GO!

We need detachment from the past. The word decision actually means to detach from something. So, growth starts with a decision. Decide to let go of something that is not allowing you to take an action and then choose a new path. Decide to take new action and create new inputs in your mind. You cannot create new things with the same considerations you had in the past. Dr. Joe Dispenza says "When you think from your past memories you can only create past experiences."

Wow, how powerful then is your mind and the thoughts you have?

How powerful can it be to acknowledge that the mindset you have can alter your entire life. Your mindset and the thoughts you have everyday will create the energetic feelings and actions that are going to empower you or disempower you. New thoughts can therefore create a new life. It will take a conscious effort to have new thoughts that will evoke new emotional energy. If you choose to have a growth mindset vs a fixed mindset, you can take on challenges in all parts of your life. If there are parts of your life that you feel are never going to change, then those very things could be your blocks and limitations.

Daily Journal Prompt:

1. What areas of your life and your identity do you feel are fixed?
2. What thoughts and beliefs will you detach from today?

Affirmation:I allow myself to let go of beliefs that were never mine. I accept myself for who I am with all the experiences I have had. I am ready to step into my true potential.

DAY 8: LACK MINDSET

Mindset is everything. Throughout my personal development journey, I always heard quotes such as, "the battle is in the mind" and "happiness depends on your mindset and attitude." Those quotes couldn't be more true. For me, my personal development journey did not create any real transformation until I realized that I had to truly take control of my mindset and the thoughts I was having. Becoming aware of the mindset that I was living in was key. I realized that I had been functioning in a lack mindset rather than an abundant mindset. As we discussed in week 1, a lack mindset tells us there is not enough and will always have us looking at what is going wrong, what we don't have, and how we are not enough. In this mindset you are not smart enough, not beautiful enough, not talented enough, not skinny enough, not rich enough, and so on. This mindset will always find the evidence for why things can never work out and, at the end of the day it casts you in the role of the victim. Here you are not taking any real control to empower yourself in creating an abundant life. The biggest evidence of a lack mindset is fear, stress, anxiousness, and constant worry. I was deeply rooted in this lack mindset for many years. And what's crazy is if you were to ask me during those years that I was sick with anxiety, if I was in gratitude, I would have told you yes. But the evidence proved otherwise. Maybe you too can reveal some parts of your life and mindset in which you are in a lack mindset rather than a mindset of abundance and gratitude.

Daily Journal Prompt:

1. What areas of your life show evidence that you may be struggling with a lack mindset?

Affirmation: I allow myself to let go of beliefs that were never mine. I accept myself for who I am with all the experiences I have had. I am ready to step into my true potential.

Day 9: The subconscious Mind

According to some studies, it is said that we have up to 50k-60k thoughts per day. Some argue that this number is not accurate, but here is what really is important to note: No matter how many thoughts per day you have, over 90% of your thoughts are the same as yesterday, and 99% of those thoughts are from your subconscious mind. Wow! This was really alarming to me and it was really important for me to become aware of this. I realized that if I was having the same thoughts as yesterday, and that the majority of those thoughts were from my deepest subconscious mind (where the negative programming and limiting beliefs lived), then I had to take control and do something. I had to really start making an effort to intentionally and consciously choose my thoughts and the emotional energy I was giving myself each day. I was becoming aware that the circumstances of my life were the result of what I was subconsciously guiding myself towards. I became aware that most of how I was acting, thinking, and behaving was because I was on autopilot. I was already programmed to react, think, and respond in a certain way based on the triggers that ignited those automatic responses. It's just like a computer program that is set up to automatically create a response when certain buttons are pushed. If I wanted to find myself in a new place then I had to rewire my subconscious mind and I had to start by making a conscious effort to do so. This is why you will hear me say, "It takes a conscious effort to win the subconscious battle" or, "It takes a conscious effort to battle the subconscious mind." Enter... the power of affirmations and words. What you think and say are creating your reality. Everything you perceive in the physical world has its origins in the invisible, inner world of your thoughts and beliefs. "As a man thinketh in his heart, so is he" Proverbs 23:7.

Can we agree that your thoughts are powerful? For me, this was a very big revelation!

Daily Journal Prompt:

1. What are some of the thoughts you have daily about life, money, love, body image, religion, God, men, women, politics, or your country that align with your current reality? Take any of these topics and choose the ones that stand out for you. Write out some statements about each that you find yourself saying or thinking when it comes to those areas of your life.
2. Once you have written those statements and thoughts, consider where in life there may be evidence that contradicts what you have written.
3. Consider that, if there is evidence that contradicts your original thoughts, could there be truth about those areas of life that would favor what you are wanting to create for your future?

Affirmation: I allow myself to let go of beliefs that were never mine. I accept myself for who I am with all the experiences I have had. I am ready to step into my true potential.

DAY 10: EMOTIONAL GUIDANCE SCALE

Congratulations you are almost half way through our first 21 day journey! Celebrate and express Gratitude! We have learned that our mindset, our thoughts, and specifically, our conscious and subconscious thoughts play a significant role on our mental health and our ability to create happiness and success in our lives. Today I want to talk with you more in depth about the power of our thoughts. You see... our thoughts are emotional energy. Every thought you have is creating an emotional energy in your body. We can easily show examples of this by thinking of a time in your life that you were hurt, betrayed, abused, or experienced something traumatic. I use the example of this time I was almost T-boned by a car while crossing an intersection. When I think about that day, my body reacts as if that moment was happening again. My heart starts to beat fast. My stomach starts to turn. And I go into this place of shock all over again. It's as if that exact event was really happening right at this moment. You see, when you think of something or choose certain thoughts, your body is really feeling it. What you will do from that moment on, whether consciously or subconsciously, is in reaction to those thoughts. If you want to feel empowered, energized, enthusiastic, strong, beautiful, and hopeful, you have to fuel your body with the right energy, and that starts with the right thoughts. I want to introduce you to the emotional guidance scale.

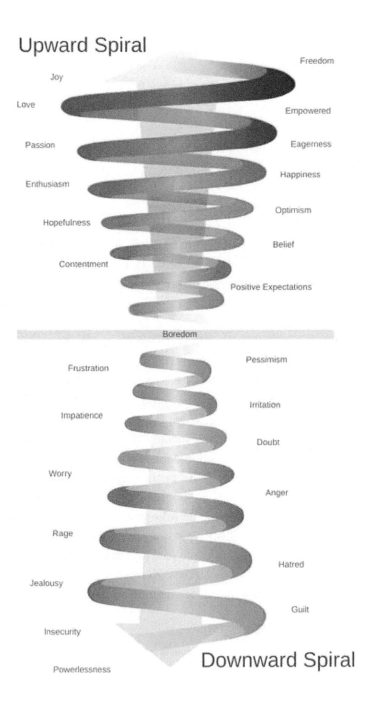

The emotional guidance scale allowed me to visualize what thoughts and feelings were pulling me either lower or higher, towards pain or towards pleasure. No... I am not saying that you should only ever feel positive or that if you ever feel any negative emotions that there is something wrong with you. There is a healthy way to feel all emotions in life, but the key is to know which emotions and thoughts are dictating and taking power over your life. Our emotions are telling us important things about our lives. For example... if you feel guilty, it does not mean you are a bad person. The emotion you are feeling is signaling you to explore how you feel and why. The key is that we don't let our daily emotions keep us defeated and stuck in life. We can own our emotions and not let those emotions own us. So... by becoming aware of this emotional guidance scale, you can determine whether your thoughts and emotions have taken over your life or not. For me, I realized quickly that I was feeding my life what is called lower energy and vibrations. But the power of choosing our thoughts gives us back control, rather than feeling like we have no control, or are stuck in situations forever. We develop a pattern of thinking as we learned on day 9. If our thoughts are the same, then we are feeling the same, and that is what is controlling our way of being. If we can consciously pull ourselves up to have more of the higher emotional thoughts, then we will feel better and I believe we can start to heal our body and mind.

Daily Journal Prompt:

1. Based on this scale, how often do you think you are functioning in a lower emotional energy throughout the day?
2. What thoughts and emotions in the higher emotional energy scale do you struggle to attain the most?

Affirmation: I allow myself to let go of beliefs that were never mine. I accept myself for who I am with all the experiences I have had. I am ready to step into my true potential.

DAY 11: LET'S TEST THE WATERS

Today I want to share with you one of my favorite experiments. You can find this on YouTube, and I highly encourage you to view it if you have never seen or heard of this experiment. It is called the 30 day rice experiment. You can also look up Dr. Emoto's awesome rice experiment. This rice experiment was started after Japanese researcher and alternative healer Dr. Masaru Emoto started to study water molecules. His research showed that human thoughts and intentions can alter the molecular structure of water. The rice experiment is done by taking two jars of cooked rice and labeling one jar "love" and the other jar "hate." For 30 days, you speak loving uplifting words to the love jar and, during those same 30 days, you speak hateful and negative words to the hate jar. What was observed after 30 days was the love jar barely even changed color, and looked as fresh as on day 1. However, the hate jar had molded and started to blacken. After conducting his water molecule research, Dr. Emoto believed that human speech and thoughts have dramatic effects on water. If that is the case, then we should be present to the fact that our bodies are made up of mostly water. About 75% of our biological tissue is water. When I heard this research, it was very much in alignment with everything I had started to read and educate myself on about the power of our thoughts. It made complete sense to me! If I was having these super low vibrational thoughts that caused negative energy, then it would make sense that my body and mind were not thriving. Instead...my body and mind were getting weaker and sicker. My body was not functioning in a thriving environment and my mind was taken over with toxic thoughts. Like mold spreads, so did my toxic thoughts. "There is life and death in the tongue." This means our words are either speaking life or they are killing us. But, do you know what is absolutely amazing? In Dr. Emoto's experiment, he took polluted water and was able to purify and clean this water by prayer and positive visualization! I believe that we can do the same with our life. If we are somewhere in life we don't want to be any longer, we can change it through our thoughts. We can purify our minds and, as one of my favorite Bible scripture says in the New living Translation: "Don't copy the behavior and customs of this world, but let God transform you into a new person by changing the way you think. Then you will learn to know God's will for you, which is good and pleasing and perfect." New international version: "Do not conform to the pattern of this world, but be transformed by the renewing of your mind. Then you will be able to test and approve what God's will is, his good, pleasing and perfect will." Romans 12:2.

Daily Journal Prompt:

1. What breakthrough did you have from learning about this water experiment?
2. Do you feel that your thoughts could be affecting your physical wellness?

Affirmation: I allow myself to let go of beliefs that were never mine. I accept myself for who I am with all the experiences I have had. I am ready to step into my true potential.

DAY 12: WHAT'S THE PATTERN?

Do you find that life for you can be like a yo-yo sometimes? Do you find it a struggle to align your goals with the actions you need to take to achieve those goals? Let's say you have always struggled financially, and there never seems to be enough money. Do you live paycheck to paycheck mostly, or do you tend to have not much left to save after paying bills? Lets say your goal is to save more and increase your financial status. You could set out a budgeting plan and a saving plan. You may even start an online side hustle to bring in more money. The first week or so, you stay on track. You are proud that you started a plan to save, and you may have even saved some money. You have been active in your side hustle; learning and starting to apply some of the ways you can earn some extra income. Things are great for a little while, but then slowly, you find it more challenging. Expenses pop up, you start to justify breaking your budget, you miss some of the activities that you used to spend money on, the side hustle is a little bit more work and discomfort than you thought, and you're not getting the success you thought you would have by now... At this point you feel defeated and start to get discouraged. Your stress hormones rise, your hope for things to change diminishes as the days go by. A few weeks or maybe a month or so later you are right back to the same place you started. This example can be used with weight loss as well.. Many people who have struggled for most of their lives with their weight find themselves right back to their overweight status after losing weight. Some may even keep it off for a few months but slowly start retreating back to where they started. You see, I was both of these people. I found myself always right back to the status I started in. I was never financially stable and, although I knew how to make a ton of money and pay off debt, I found myself right back in debt and struggling financially. After college and having kids I started struggling with my weight, and year after year, my weight would go up and down. I would lose weight then gain it right back. I followed that pattern over and over. The reason why this happened is because I had already attached myself to a story of who I was, and what life would be like for me. I was also subconsciously comfortable with those identities and stories. We don't realize that over time, we grow attached to the stories we tell over and over. My story was always about how I grew up poor and how my family doesn't have the skinny genes. I would say things like, "I never had a fast metabolism" and, "I just love food so much". My relationship to money was that it was never available or we always had too little. These stories were a way of life for me. Unconsciously, I was making my story a reality over and over. My identity became that I was poor and that I don't stand a chance to ever really be fit and skinny. Although consciously I wanted to be financially wealthy, and physically healthy and fit, my subconscious belief was saying the opposite. This was why my life was a yo-yo. Here is where you will notice that, slowly, your actions will cease to align with the intentions you set out to create. The more you can expand your awareness the more you can expand your possibilities.

Daily Journal Prompt:

1. Would you say there is alignment with your desires and the actions you take regularly?
2. What are the patterns you find yourself in?
3. What stories about yourself must change now in order for your goals to manifest?

Affirmation: I allow myself to let go of beliefs that were never mine. I accept myself for who I am with all the experiences I have had. I am ready to step into my true potential.

DAY 13: VICTIM MINDSET

Today we will further expand on the lack mindset and dig down to another layer within this malignant state of mind. I remember when I first started to learn about what a victim mindset really was. I became super conscious that there were parts of my life in which I was playing the victim card. I believe that for most people, they are doing the same without realizing it. For some, they are ok with being the victim, and actually justify this lack of responsibility in that specific area of their life. But here is the hard truth, and most find it hard to believe and accept: It is never ok to be the victim in any situation. You can take full responsibility for your present and future. Simply put, the victim can never be a victor. The two do not align. A victim is never taking control. Rather, a victim is the one being controlled. The victim will always find the events, circumstances, weaknesses, excuses, problems, and the reasons why they can't do or have what they want. Life's circumstances are always going to be somebody else's fault or responsibility. Victims regularly predict defeat or give up quickly, and rarely believe that things will work out. Victims complain about how things are being handled and create very "understandable" excuses for not taking any action or responsibility. It's never their fault, rather, their parents, their teachers, the government, their spouse, partner, their boss, their friends, and so on. Victims also tend to compare themselves to others or find ways in which they lack skills or talents. They love to use their circumstances or discuss how someone else has it better or has more available resources than they do. In a victim mindset, the focus is on what they don't want or on problems that constantly preoccupy their lives. Victims can find themselves living in fear and feeling a loss of purpose.

I learned quickly that if my mind and energy were ever in alignment with a victim mindset, I could never focus on and create what I desired. I could actually choose wisely and take aligned actions to achieve the life I wanted. I realized I had to accept personal responsibility to create a new life that is different from what I had. I would never have to settle for anything less. It is up to us to catch ourselves when we feel that the victim mindset is setting in. We can choose consciously to make the right choices and look for actions we can take to prevent us from being the victim moving forward.

Daily Journal Prompt:

1. Where in life may you have found yourself settling?
2. Why may you have chosen to settle in that area of your life?
3. What could you create for yourself by taking on a creator mindset vs a victim mindset?

Affirmation: I allow myself to let go of beliefs that were never mine. I accept myself for who I am with all the experiences I have had. I am ready to step into my true potential.

DAY 14: WHAT TRIGGERS YOU?

As you continue revealing, unraveling, and becoming more aware about who you are and the identities you have taken on that are not authentic to you, we need to discuss the topic of triggers.

"Triggers reveal to us the areas of our life where we are not free". Our emotional triggers are not just about the situations and things around us that we find unpleasant or annoying or frustrating. They are actually telling us about something that is happening in relation to our self worth, our self acceptance, our confidence, our limitations, and more. Triggers are revealing to us aspects in our life where we lack freedom and satisfaction. Epictetus, the philosopher said, "People are disturbed not by things, but by their views of things." As we have discovered earlier on, our view of life is filtered through beliefs and identities rooted in our subconscious minds. The experiences we've had, the stories we've been told, the things we've heard said to us by our parents and other influencers in our lives. We have put on filters to view things and how we think about those things. The way we feel about ourselves determines the reactions we will have to those triggers. Those triggers could be revealing the need to heal from a past trauma, they may remind us of past relationships, or events that didn't leave a positive impact in our lives where we need closure. Triggers come in many forms. Triggers can be places, people, noises, sounds, beliefs, opinions, and more.

While doing this work, I discovered that the very root issue of triggers really comes down to the consequence of having a fixed mindset, and again the lack mindset. I'll explain why. You see... triggers are rooted in our perception of the world and our understanding of the world (which is linked to our thoughts and beliefs). These beliefs are also attached to our stories and experiences. We translate and create these beliefs and stories in our own way, and when we close our minds to seeing things any other way, then we will forever be triggered when something around us is different from us, or contradicts our beliefs. If we become attached to only one way of thinking, then of course a different way of being or thinking is going to trigger us. It's always going to be easier to accept people and things that are similar to who we are and how we do things. If someone goes against our beliefs, we feel attacked and we will feel the need to be defensive. I have learned that the reasons I have been triggered is because I was in a place where I had to question my own beliefs or ways of thinking, which was not comfortable. Now… this does not mean you have to change or give up your beliefs. The freedom lies when you don't allow the discomfort to take over, accept that you are ok, and that it is ok that others have a different view on things. That should have no impact on your beliefs if you choose to keep your beliefs. If someone says you are ugly and you get all heated and fired up and upset... that is when the trigger took over. But if you are free to think and know that someone's opinion about you doesn't hold any truth to you and it's just their own belief, then you will not let that person's opinion of you have this negative effect on you.

Daily Journal Prompt:

1. What are you present to when it comes to the things that trigger you?
2. What may be the reasons you feel those triggers?

Affirmation: I allow myself to let go of beliefs that were never mine. I accept myself for who I am with all the experiences I have had. I am ready to step into my true potential.

DAY 15: YOUR RITUALS

Most people may think that rituals are only specific practices and observations that are tied to beliefs or religion. We tend to think of rituals as something you have to create and design and apply daily in order to attain an end goal. For some, it's the lifestyle practice for freedom and happiness. But the truth is... we all have rituals. A ritual is simply just what you practice regularly. Your rituals are either working for you or not. You see... if everyday you wake up and you do the same things within the first hour of waking up, then that has become your morning ritual. For many, it looks similar. Most people wake up, grab their cell phones and check their notifications, emails, social media, ect. They may have started first by snoozing their alarms a few times before actually waking up. The next steps could be making coffee and hopping on social media again while sipping their morning brew. For some, it could be turning on the TV to catch the news. For those who have kids, it's a crazy rush of gathering children, making breakfast, preparing lunches for school, ect. Whatever the case, the point is, we all have morning and daily rituals. The things we are choosing to do each day and the activities we participate in throughout the day are all creating our present realities. Those rituals are working for you or they are not. The definition of insanity is doing the same thing over and over and expecting different results. If we truly want to achieve our goals and manifest more abundance, health, love, and freedom, then it starts with creating new rituals and habits. Changing your morning ritual is something I highly advise. If you have made it this far into the book, you may have already started that commitment. Starting your day with gratitude is highly recommended. Establishing a healthy morning ritual sets the tone for the day. It will energize you and build focus and intentions for the day, and align you with what you desire to see happen. It also allows you to start taking control of your day rather than letting the day take control of you. A morning ritual that involves nourishing your body, mind, and spirit will create more peace and clarity for you. Your morning ritual does not have to look like anyone else's. You can design a morning ritual of your own. It can involve prayer and meditation, stretching, journaling, or listening to affirmations. There are a ton of resources today that you can plug into to create your perfect morning ritual.

Daily Journal Prompt:

1. What has been your morning ritual?
2. Do you desire to have a better daily ritual? If so, how would that look for you?
3. Do you find that your day takes control of you? What part of your days do you feel are chaotic? How could that change?

Affirmation: I allow myself to let go of beliefs that were never mine. I accept myself for who I am with all the experiences I have had. I am ready to step into my true potential.

DAY 16: IT'S NO JOKE

I recently read a very interesting article once about the dangers and consequences of jokes that are denigrating. For example... expressions of prejudice in a cloak of fun and humor are actually not harmless, but can foster discrimination against targeted groups. Disparaging humor can negatively affect people's understanding of social norms and much more. So why do I bring this up? Well, many of us use humor and jokes that are self-deprecating, finding it funny to do so. Simple examples: I am so dumb. Anyone else hate themselves too? Anyone else always manage to never get it right? Of course I didn't get that right. I'm always a disaster, etc. Many of these types of jokes are made into memes and graphics and shared. Research has shown that being openly negative about yourself, even if done in a humorous way, has a detrimental effect on your mental health and can negatively affect your professional success. Jokes like these can be about anxiety, depression, money, health, food, love, sex, and more. But when the jokes are pessimistic, negative, or degrading, they are perpetuating thoughts and beliefs that are in conflict with what we truly desire to manifest and create. It all goes back to revealing what is truly at the root of our subconscious beliefs and how they are in alignment or not with what we are working to create.

Daily Journal Prompt:

1. What types of things do you find yourself saying in a humorous way that is in total conflict with what you want to believe and align with?

Affirmation: I allow myself to let go of beliefs that were never mine. I accept myself for who I am with all the experiences I have had. I am ready to step into my true potential.

DAY 17: WHAT YOU FEED GROWS

I love this Native American parable:

An old Cherokee is teaching his grandson about life. "A fight is going on inside me," he said to the boy. "It is a terrible fight and it is between two wolves. One is evil – he is anger, envy, sorrow, regret, greed, arrogance, self-pity, guilt, resentment, inferiority, lies, false pride, superiority, and ego."

He continued, "The other is good – he is joy, peace, love, hope, serenity, humility, kindness, benevolence, empathy, generosity, truth, compassion, and faith. The same fight is going on inside you – and inside every other person, too". The grandson thought about it for a minute and then asked his grandfather, "Which wolf will win?" The old Cherokee simply replied, "The one you feed."

There is so much we can learn from this parable and I believe it serves as such a great reminder that everyday we are feeding ourselves the right thoughts or the wrong thoughts. "What you focus on grows, what you think about expands, and what you dwell upon determines your destiny." - Robin S. Sharma.

Daily Journal Prompt:

1. Using the parable as an example of our internal battles, describe your internal battle. What do your two wolves stand for? Which do you want to feed more?

Affirmation: I allow myself to let go of beliefs that were never mine. I accept myself for who I am with all the experiences I have had. I am ready to step into my true potential.

DAY 18: WHAT IS YOUR PRIORITY?

Every day you make decisions and you make choices. Those decisions and choices make up your life. At the end of the day, those decisions and choices are tied to your priorities. Some simple examples of priorities are as follows: You prioritize feeding your children because it's a non-negotiable responsibility that you know you must do to be a good parent. You also may choose to take a shower and brush your teeth everyday. That choice is a priority because you value the importance of being clean and practicing good hygiene. Again... this is a non-negotiable. You may decide that you want to start organizing a messy closet or take on a DIY project. You decide this because again, you may value and prioritize organization, so you spend a good amount of time throughout the day cleaning and organizing your house. Simply put, we all have our priorities and no-negotiables. For most of us, it will not matter what happens throughout the day, we will always find time for our priorities. The things that are priorities become non-negotiables. You see, you never have to negotiate with your priorities. At the end of the day you will always take actions on the things you value and tie a high level of importance too. So, just like feeding your children, taking showers, and brushing your teeth are non-negotiables, you can create new priorities and non-negotiables that align specifically with your future goals. Once you create these new priorities and set them at a high value, you will learn that they eventually become non-negotiables. They become daily lifestyle practices, and as we discussed earlier, they become your rituals that develop the systems and practices that bring you in alignment with your goals. Your goals could be related to health, money, communication, leadership, or career. Whatever the long term goals are, you can create your new priorities and non-negotiables that tie into these. Once you prioritize them, you will see how you will always manage to take actions that will align you with those goals.

What you find yourself making time for everyday is a reflection of what your true priorities are in life. As we discussed in week 1... if you are not careful, you will find yourself always staying in your comfort zone settling for mediocrity.

Daily Journal Prompt:

1. What are your current priorities?
2. How are your daily actions and rituals in alignment with your priorities?
3. What actions and rituals could you create that will bring you closer to your goals?

Affirmation: I allow myself to let go of beliefs that were never mine. I accept myself for who I am with all the experiences I have had. I am ready to step into my true potential.

DAY 19: SELF DOUBT

Achieving your goals can be instantly stopped by one simple emotion... Doubt. If you ever feel doubt about the possibility of actually achieving your goals and desires, this very emotion will disempower you and place you instantly in a lower emotional energy. In turn, this is creating conflicts within the feelings and thoughts about what you are trying to manifest. You see... the expectation of receiving a specific result is what gives us the motivation to act. And for many of us, we can easily find ourselves in a sea of doubt because of past experiences of not achieving the results we wanted. We may also see evidence of the lack of results others are receiving, and or we hear the stories from others about their lack of results. We could also be setting ourselves up for the wrong expectations and stress about how or when the results will come and therefore falling again into a sea of doubt. The second we begin to doubt is the moment our energies shift in the wrong alignment. Doubt shifts us into a lack mindset where we are looking and wondering why the things we desire are not coming or have not come yet. This energy gets us demotivated and does not inspire the actions we should take to stay in the alignment we need. Doubt will have us comparing ourselves to others and doesn't allow us to be grateful for what we currently have at this moment. Doubt shifts things to be seen as bad vs good, which creates conflict. When there is conflict in your mind, you can not be at peace because you are now concerned about the outcome. All this happens with that evil little emotion called doubt. But you see... when you lack nothing and you have no doubt about the outcome, your energy and thoughts are filled with confidence. You are more empowered and motivated.

Daily Journal Prompt:

1. Where in your life can you see where self doubt has kept you from achieving a goal?
2. Are you present to how self doubt demotivates you from taking actions towards your goals?
3. What areas in your life do you want to stop doubting yourself?

Affirmation: I allow myself to let go of beliefs that were never mine. I accept myself for who I am with all the experiences I have had. I am ready to step into my true potential.

DAY 20: SELF CONTROL

So much of our successes and achievements are built on our daily actions, our rituals, our choices, our good habits, and as we just learned, our priorities. In order to achieve these things we must have self control and discipline to consistently show up for ourselves and take the actions we say we will take. We must also refrain from the bad habits we have made in the past. If in the past we have lacked a lot of self control to refrain from bad habits, then self awareness is essential in this area. Being aware that there is a present struggle with self control means intentionally creating a plan to support yourself in shifting your normal ways of being. It is also important to have self awareness of your level of self control. In these first 21 days we are unraveling and revealing so we can heal and not disregard our emotions, triggers, and unhealthy behaviors. Remember... it takes a conscious effort to battle the subconscious. When we are working on auto-pilot and are easily programmed to react and respond in a certain way, we have to make a lot of conscious and intentional decisions to help us create a new way of being. Our emotional awareness is key to understanding why we feel the way we feel and why we do the things we do. Most of the reasons we lack self control in our lives could be linked specifically to a feeling of lack or freedom in our lives. My goal with this workbook is to help you feel more freedom and fulfillment in who you are once you strip away all the parts of you that keep you unfulfilled and lacking. Once you are fully in alignment with your true authentic self and realize you have way more control of your thoughts and decisions, you will be a master of your emotions and therefore have discipline and self control. The next 21 days will guide you to a deeper level of self awareness as you discover what self love and forgiveness truly means and what it can do for your confidence and motivation in achieving your life goals.

Daily Journal Prompt:

1. How confident do you feel in your ability to have self control to create new habits and new rituals?

Affirmation: I allow myself to let go of beliefs that were never mine. I accept myself for who I am with all the experiences I have had. I am ready to step into my true potential.

DAY 21: SELF AWARENESS

Congratulations you are now completing your first 21 days. I pray you can see yourself more clearly, that you have started a journey of receiving more clarity about your goals and desires, and that you can see the things that took hold of you and were holding you back. The identity you took on that was keeping you inauthentic is no longer there. The stories and meanings you attached about life, money, love, success, health that were not true are now leaving. You now have a conscious awareness of the thoughts you had on a regular basis and how those things may have been disempowering you. You now know the triggers and emotions that help reveal to you the parts of your life that lacked freedom and full expression. You can now step into a new possibility of becoming a person who has more conscious awareness of the thoughts and actions that will override the old programming and old patterns and old ways of being. Today, you step into a new way of being with new possibilities and with nothing from the past. Now, you step into a place where you lack nothing and can see yourself as someone who has control over your thoughts and actions. You have the belief that you are worthy and fully capable of achieving your goals and desires. Today you begin your self love journey. These next 21 days will move you further into alignment of fulfillment and love, which is crucial to manifesting the health and love and abundance you desire. If you are taking actions and creating new rituals, you must create from a place of wholeness and love. If you are only taking actions to escape from reality and pain, rather than reconnecting to your true essence, then you will never feel satisfied. It will never matter what you have or own or look like if you are not loving yourself where you are. If you are never grateful for what you have then you will never be or have enough.

Daily Journal Prompt:

1. What old beliefs and thoughts are no longer going to take part in your future?

Affirmation: I allow myself to let go of beliefs that were never mine. I accept myself for who I am with all the experiences I have had. I am ready to step into my true potential.

Part 2: Love

DAY 22: WHAT IS SELF LOVE?

What does it mean to have true self love? Self love is layers deep, just like our own life, and just like our journey in personal development. There are so many layers of understanding your ways of being. Many of us have surface level ideas as an interpretation of what self love means. But, it is super important to note that self love is the highest and most powerful love you can practice to truly step into freedom in all areas of your life.

Loving yourself isn't only about pampering yourself and doing things like a night out, watching your favorite show at night, taking baths, shopping, or getting a spa treatment. Self love isn't just taking actions to make you feel good; rather, self love is an inside job.

When you love yourself fully because you know you are whole and complete and made perfect in God's image. When you have no shame or guilt from past mistakes. When you receive and give forgiveness, love, compassion, appreciation and more, that's when you will naturally desire to treat yourself kindly. Receiving God's love and stepping into the power of the truest and highest love we were given will deliver you to a place where you will exude love, compassion, and gratitude. You are detached from any external things, or people to make you feel worthy. You know your worth and value and set your standards high and your life on the outside will be an overflow of the love you have inside. This work can only be done by first accepting and receiving God's love. No one can receive it for you. It's a step you must take yourself. Remembering who you are through God's eyes. Stepping into your true essence. This doesn't mean that you wont make mistakes or fail but it means that you are loved either way. It's understanding that even with your imperfections and flaws you are loved by your creator and there is no need to receive anything else besides that unfailing love that is available to you and for you always.

When you can see yourself in this beautiful way, you become confident and your desires and actions reflect how you feel on the inside. When the inside job is done, you give your body what it needs physically, mentally, and spiritually. Your body is a temple and how you treat yourself and how you allow others to treat you is a reflection of that inside work.

Daily Journal Prompt:

1. What are the actions you do right now that reflect the self love you have?
2. What personal routines do you have that reflect self love?
3. What areas of your life are you present to that lack a reflection of love you have not received?

Affirmation: I am worthy. I am complete. I am valuable. I am loved. I am powerful. I am strong. I am a super conqueror.

DAY 23: YOUR SELF WORTH

I have been in an industry the past 6 years in which 99% of the business is made up of women. I have had the pleasure to lead and train and work with beautiful women, and it's been an incredible experience. I love working with women who are goal oriented and driven. However, a common issue that many women seem to share is a lack of self worth. On the external and conscious level many women will say they feel worthy of success, or they desire to create beautiful abundant relationships, careers, and businesses. Deep down, however, they struggle with a true sense of self worth. Somewhere deep down these women lost their sense of true value and worth. They settled for relationships, careers, and businesses that are just average or mediocre. This self worth issue can lead women into comparing themselves to other women. It will have women constantly worried about what others think of them, and worst of all, it keeps women in toxic and unhealthy relationships. In summary, having self worth issues will be one of the biggest blocks to truly stepping into your self love journey. Some of the root causes of our low self esteem and self worth issues started with our childhood environment. Our parents, or close friends and family and their behaviors towards us have a major impact on our self esteem and self worth. Loss, trauma, and rejection also have a profound impact on our self worth. This is an important area of your life where I highly encourage you to spend time in. Unravel past or even recent events, relationships, and circumstances that have maybe played a role and been the cause of any possible self worth issues you may or may not have been present to. Do you have a critic inside of you that speaks negatively? Does the inner critic tell you life is too hard and you are always struggling, that you don't matter, that you are not good enough or smart enough? Unraveling your self talk, and the thoughts you have about your worth and connecting those to a root cause will give you the power to take control.

After all, in the end we alone are responsible for how we perceive ourselves.

Daily Journal Prompt:

1. List the areas of your life in which you feel worthy of?
2. What desires do you feel not worthy of?
3. What root causes of your low self worth are you present to?

Affirmation: I am worthy. I am complete. I am valuable. I am loved. I am powerful. I am strong. I am a super conqueror.

DAY 24: COMPARISON IS THE THIEF OF JOY

Lacking self love will find us victims of comparison. Comparison, as we have learned from earlier weeks, lives within a lack mindset, but above all, it is evidence that we are lacking self love. It will be easy to compare ourselves to others when we don't feel secure, worthy, and confident in who we are and what we have. When we lack clarity in what we want and why we are doing it then we will always question ourselves and look externally for the things we feel we should be doing, feeling, or having. If we lack discernment and intuition we will easily be swayed and influenced by what others are doing. We have all heard of the saying, "keeping up with the Jones's." And my goodness… trying to keep up with the Jones's is going to get exhausting. Comparison will never ever allow you to be enough or have enough. There will always be someone or something you are going to think is better than you, and you are going to find yourself constantly feeling lack. This does not allow you to ever feel complete and free. Comparison is the effect of the lack of self love you have for who you are and is also the effect of the lack of clarity you have about your desires and your calling in life. When you can truly step into self love, you will give yourself this freedom and fulfillment of knowing you are complete, and you can focus more on being in alignment and discernment. You will find your gifts and talents, and you will focus on flourishing those gifts. You will do the actions that make you feel more joyful and happy. Your focus shifts to gratitude and abundance rather than looking outside at what others are doing, leaving you always feeling like you don't have enough. Remember that there is only one you. You will always make a lousy someone else but you will make a great YOU. Focus on your personal journey and look for ways to flourish your path with experiences and people who will add so much value to who you are.

Daily Journal Prompt:

1. In what areas of your life do you find yourself comparing to others?
2. What areas of your life are you super proud of?

Affirmation: I am worthy. I am complete. I am valuable. I am loved. I am powerful. I am strong. I am a super conqueror.

DAY 25: STOP THE SHAME AND GUILT

Shame and guilt are both something I highly encourage you to let go of and cut cords with. Shame and guilt will always make you feel less and will always have you look at yourself in a negative way. These feelings will not allow you to feel the love for yourself you need to thrive in life. You can choose to take control of this area of your life if you are struggling with shame and guilt.

You may feel shame in your life for actions or decisions you made that you feel went against the social norms you believe in. Shame may make you feel embarrassed, humiliated, and have you keeping your head down vs your head up. It conflicts with self confidence and your pride, and most importantly, it affects your self esteem.

Guilt combines the feeling of shame, anxiety and humiliation. And just like shame, guilt can affect our self worth and self esteem. Lingering guilt and shame in your life will keep you from truly enjoying life. It will impede your productivity, your rest, your creativity, and more. Studies have shown that if you have unresolved guilt and shame in your life, you're spending many hours a week having feelings of guilt. As we learned earlier, our thoughts are affecting our bodies. Imagine how much we are hurting ourselves by having thoughts of guilt and shame on a daily basis. The following journal prompts have personally helped me release shame and guilt in areas of my life I was struggling with.

Daily Journal Prompt:

1. Journal about the things you feel shame and guilt on.
2. Write down why you feel shame and guilt about those things.
3. Talk about it with someone. It's amazing what happens when you share and bring things to the light with someone else. If you are not

ready to share, write a letter as if you were going to give it to the person.

4. Be honest with yourself and don't ever pretend it never happened. Accept what has happened and know that it is in the past and you will no longer carry it into the future.

5. Talk to the person or persons you may have some unresolved issues with that may be causing your feelings of guilt. Again if you are not ready to talk, write a letter to that person.

Affirmation: I am worthy. I am complete. I am valuable. I am loved. I am powerful. I am strong. I am a super conqueror.

DAY 26: THE F WORD

My favorite F word is Forgiveness. It was the most transformational action that upgraded my life and allowed me to truly feel happy and to manifest even more love and happiness into my life. If you are holding onto unforgiveness for yourself and for others, it's the biggest block of all to your goals and desires. I encourage you to step into the possibility of true forgiveness everyday until it finally takes hold. Understand it's not always going to happen overnight. Allow yourself to let the past go, and the pain and hurt go. Choose to live in the present moment, and choose to have the vision of the future that you are creating. Nothing from the past can infiltrate your new future. So, if you are allowing unforgiveness in your heart from past events into your present, it will be a heavy ball and chain tied to you. Giving forgiveness to yourself and others is one of the biggest ways you can practice self love for yourself. Forgiveness will allow you to stop beating yourself up and will stop you from feeling all the guilt and shame you think about. You will respect yourself and accept yourself which will empower yourself more to take actions and behaviors that are healthy for you. Also… if you are not forgiving others and holding on to resentment and anger for those who hurt you, you are really hurting yourself. Being able to forgive others says that you are enough, that love is abundant, and that even though we may have been wronged, we don't have to spend the rest of our lives robbing ourselves of joy and healing and growth. I promise that if you can let it go, you are going to open the doors to so much amazing abundance that wants to come in, and those are the things that truly matter.

Daily Journal Prompt:

1. What areas of your life are you holding unforgiveness in?
2. What does forgiveness mean to you?
3. What are some ways you can be more forgiving?
4. Do you believe people who are forgiving are happier?

Affirmation: I am worthy. I am complete. I am valuable. I am loved. I am powerful. I am strong. I am a super conqueror.

DAY 27: SELF COMPASSION

How often are you practicing self compassion? Self compassion is a great way to allow your behaviors and actions to reflect and align with the self love you need to feel more joyful and proud of yourself. In return, this becomes a great recipe for manifesting amazing relationships and opportunities for success in your life. Self compassion allows you also to have compassion for others and be more understanding and kind. When having compassion for others you understand that suffering and failure and imperfections are part of the human experience, and it's ok. When you practice this type of compassion for yourself you will be kind to yourself and give yourself the grace and love and forgiveness you are deserving of. You will not be hard on yourself and belittle yourself for trying to meet some crazy impossible and unrealistic standard of perfection. Self compassion allows you to never ever look at yourself as worthless or unacceptable when you try new things and fail a couple of times. You understand it's ok to fail and that failure doesn't mean you are a failure in life. Self compassion allows you to step into a place where you accept who you are and all the human aspects of you. Things will not always go the way you planned, and it's ok. You will experience anger, frustration, mistakes, and loss, but you are not alone in this, and it's a reality for all human beings. The more you stop resisting failures and mistakes, the more freedom you will feel in life. So, be gentle on yourself, and remember you are not alone in your challenges. The human experience is all the same.

Daily Journal Prompt:

1. List some areas of your life that you have held to a very high standard and are not giving yourself the compassion you need?
2. What parts of who you are can you be more gentle with?
3. List the parts of you who you are and skills you have that you are grateful for.

Affirmation: I am worthy. I am complete. I am valuable. I am loved. I am powerful. I am strong. I am a super conqueror.

DAY 28: WHERE YOUR FOCUS GOES ENERGY FLOWS

I want to discuss with you today about the reticular activating system also known as the RAS. The reticular activator in our brain is a bundle of nerves at our brainstem that filters out unnecessary information so that the important stuff gets through. Your RAS takes what you focus on and helps you find the evidence for it. And as the famous quote says, "Whether you think you can or you think you can't, you are right." Your RAS will always seek out information to validate your beliefs. The RAS helps you to see what you want to see and what you believe is real, and because we know that thoughts influence our feelings then those beliefs and thoughts will influence the actions we take to align with the beliefs we have. So what does this have to do with self love? Well it's very simple. If on a daily basis your focus and the thoughts about yourself are not in alignment with what you want to feel, then your energy and emotions will always pull you to feel what you are focusing on. And those negative emotions are influencing the actions you take or do not take. This is why for example instead of eating healthier, exercising, getting dressed up more often, or pampering yourself, you will feel unmotivated and lack any reason to care for yourself. If you feel negatively about yourself, then your focus and energy goes to showing you evidence of why you are all of those negative things you say about yourself. You will find yourself justifying why you are the way you are and why you can't be any other way, and then you will find more external reasons to justify these beliefs. The people around you will start to treat you in the way you allow yourself to be treated and will give back in return exactly what you expect. Your focus is on all the wrong things. But if you shift your focus on all the ways you want to feel and the new personality you want to have then you can create just that. Your new focus will create a new source of energy and alignment, and it will fuel your new actions and behaviors. Sooner or later the environment around you begins to change because first you changed your focus.

Daily Journal Prompt:

1. What do you focus on mostly when it comes to your skills, your body and health, or your life?
2. Where has your focus been lately?
3. What new evidence for your life will you now choose to have your RAS focus on?

Affirmation: I am worthy. I am complete. I am valuable. I am loved. I am powerful. I am strong. I am a super conqueror.

DAY 29: OLD YOU OR NEW YOU?

"Most of you won't be successful, not because you can't do it, but because you can't outlast your Old you long enough to get to your New you." - Eric Thomas. This quote resonates so deeply with me. I love this perspective about success, because when you really start to dig deeper into the personal development journey, you become more aware that all the blocks and limitations set on us have everything to do with the deep programming and beliefs ingrained in our subconscious minds that are part of our past. What we call the old self. We have this old way of being, thinking, and feeling that must cease to exist in order for a new us to emerge. The new you must be, think, and feel differently then you have been, otherwise you create the same future as the past. If your self-talk has been telling you that you are not good enough, smart enough, pretty enough, handsome enough, young enough, healthy enough, rich enough, and the list goes on, then you are creating a self fulfilling prophecy. As the quote above says, you will never outlast your old you long enough to get to your new you. For many of us, we will have to face that limiting destructive self-talk we hear in our heads that wants to keep us in fear and in our comfort zone by telling us we are not good enough or lucky enough to have a new life. Maybe you have found all the reasons why you feel you can not do something. If your focus has led you to find evidence all around to justify those behaviors and beliefs, then you may be so deeply rooted in your old ways and patterns that you are finding it hard to step into a new way of being. I am here to tell you, yes it will be hard, but I am also here to remind you that you can do hard things. I encourage you to create a new self-talk that steps into love everyday and lets you outlast the old you so the new you is all that is left. One step forward each day. That's all you need to do until you have walked miles into your future self.

Daily Journal Prompt:

1. What does your old self say about what you can or can't do?
2. What does your new self say?

Affirmation: I am worthy. I am complete. I am valuable. I am loved. I am powerful. I am strong. I am a super conqueror.

DAY 30: WHAT'S ON REPLAY?

Today I want to share something my dear friend, Jenny Wallman, once wrote:

"We tell ourselves stories on a continuous loop and often we don't even realize how much we talk to ourselves. Here are a few of my stories:

You're such a bad mom. You look like a troll. You're failing at everything. You are not a good leader. You don't have the ability to show love. You're such a dumpster fire. Wow, that's harsh. And those are just a few. In the shower this morning I started running down the list and stopped myself abruptly. Holy Cow Y'all, I would never, and I mean never, say any of these things to anyone else. And if I did, I'd bet I'd have approximately zero friends. So why do I treat myself this horribly? Well I can assure you it ends today. I am on a mission to fully love myself and treat myself like I was my best friend. Because I deserve that. And the stories that play on repeat... I am going to rewrite them. I am becoming the best version of myself, finding my identity, and ending this chapter of self destruction. Are you with me?"

Daily Journal Prompt:

1. What has been on replay in your mind and thoughts?
2. What repeat emotions and feelings show up for you daily?
3. What will you rewrite today?

Affirmation: I am worthy. I am complete. I am valuable. I am loved. I am powerful. I am strong. I am a super conqueror.

DAY 31: YOU DESERVE IT

Your life is evidence of what you feel you deserve and what you believe is available for you. We are constantly in communication with God, our environment, and people around us about what we are willing to have, tolerate, and receive. How we show up, dress, behave, act, take, give, respond, react, and speak are all communicating something. If you are not happy with the way things currently are in your life, consider what you may be communicating about those areas of your life and what you believe you are deserving of. Practicing self love is taking massive action to embody the love and blessings you truly believe you deserve. When you believe you are not good enough you behave as if it was true, as if it was evidence. So you behave and interact in a way that confirms what you believe. As a result, others treat you that way too. When you align with giving love to yourself, you manifest more love and abundance right back to you. Today, start believing you are deserving.

Daily Journal Prompt:

1. What are some ways you are showing up that communicate the opposite of what you are looking to manifest?
2. In which ways may you be acting, thinking, speaking, behaving, or even dressing, that do not communicate how and what you really want to feel and desire in life?

Affirmation: I am worthy. I am complete. I am valuable. I am loved. I am powerful. I am strong. I am a super conqueror.

DAY 32: NON-NEGOTIABLE

Self Care is one of the top priorities we should have among the things in our life that are non-negotiable. Recharging our bodies and our minds is essential to living a healthy and thriving life. You would never go a day without charging your phone. If you use your computer for daily work activities you would never let your computer not recharge regularly. The majority of us today would never think to not have our chargers with us when traveling because we know that our phones and devices will need to charge. Well our bodies and minds are the same. It is an essential part of life yet many of us are running on empty and barely taking time to recharge our minds and our bodies. I also believe that our bodies must charge and connect with God our creator who is our source of life and knowledge. Plugging into our creator daily keeps us fueled with love and gratitude and keeps our discernment in check. Self care and recharging your mind and body will lead to higher productivity and will give you more clarity in making decisions. Self care is a way to love yourself and make yourself a priority which improves your self compassion and restores your energy by focusing on what you need. If your mind is always cluttered and overwhelmed with feeling like you have to constantly take care of everyone else but yourself, you're actually depleting your energy, mental stability, and discernment. Self care allows you to improve your relationships and communication with your family, friends, and co-workers. Self care recharges you so you can give and take care of your responsibilities better than you would when you're running on empty. Make self care non-negotiable in your life.

Daily Journal Prompt:

1. Has self care been a non-negotiable for you?
2. What are some ways you can prioritize self care into your routines?
3. What holds you back from self care?
4. Are those reasons rooted in lack or abundance?

Affirmation: I am worthy. I am complete. I am valuable. I am loved. I am powerful. I am strong. I am a super conqueror.

DAY 33: GIVE YOURSELF GRACE

Forgiveness has a cousin and her name is Grace. Grace is a really great companion to have around. She's kind and understanding and always loving. Grace accepts you right where you are at even on your messiest and most challenging days. She heals you and lets you put yourself back together when you have those moments of breakdowns. Grace never makes you feel like a failure when you make one too many mistakes or when the laundry has been piled up on the couch for a week. Grace extends self compassion and never judges you when you feel any sense of guilt. Grace helps you deal with your fear of failure and gives you permission to do it messy and imperfectly. Grace never gives you a hard time for not meeting crazy expectations that you set for yourself. And you know that mean girl or boy that likes to stick around sometimes? The one that is super hard on you. The one who tells you how you are not good enough, pretty enough, handsome enough, smart enough, skilled enough, or that you have no talent… Grace deals with them kindly as well, and she's so much stronger than that mean girl or boy. When you bring Grace around more often the mean ones don't come around as much, and eventually, they stop coming around ever. Grace loves to talk about your amazing talents and gifts and accomplishments. She is super generous with her compliments and loves to tell you how unique and amazing you are, and how deserving you are. I encourage you to bring her around as often as you can.

Daily Journal Prompt:

1. What does Grace say about you that you love to hear?
2. How often do you bring Grace around?

Affirmation: I am worthy. I am complete. I am valuable. I am loved. I am powerful. I am strong. I am a super conqueror.

DAY 34: VULNERABILITY IS ENDEARING

If you are like me, you may have at least one social media account or, for some of us, multiple social accounts. And like many on social media, people tend to post what I call "highlight reels" of their life. Most of us dare not post the things that we don't want people to know about us in fear of losing likes, friends, or being judged. We put on filters, and post beautiful fun images and videos. But one thing I have realized in my personal development and growth journey is that, it is in my most vulnerable moments that I have been able to connect the most with people. Vulnerability is endearing because it allows us all to be ok in our weaknesses and confusion. Vulnerability allows us to be human with one another. Vulnerability actually creates a safe environment to fully be present and be ok with messing up and not having to meet really crazy expectations. It's ok to not always know what you are doing and confessing it to yourself and to others. There is freedom in vulnerability. Vulnerability allows you to relate and connect with others who fail, make mistakes, and admit that they need help... just like you. Pretending to always know how to figure things out with no one else's help, or pretending that everything is perfect when it's not is exhausting. Vulnerability is the truest form of connection. Vulnerability empowers you to foster courage and strength with not just yourself, but with others around you.

Daily Journal Prompt:

1. What is your relationship with vulnerability?
2. Does being vulnerable make you feel a certain way?
3. How can you change the way that vulnerability looks for you now that is different then what it looked like in the past?

4. What areas of life are you vulnerable in that you may not share or keep from others?

Affirmation: I am worthy. I am complete. I am valuable. I am loved. I am powerful. I am strong. I am a super conqueror.

DAY 35: MIRROR MIRROR ON THE WALL

I used to have a very unhealthy relationship with mirrors. Being in front of mirrors were times where I would hate on myself more than love on myself. Now... were there times when I looked in the mirror and complemented myself? Yes there were some times, but even when I complimented myself it was always followed by wishing some other part of me was better. For example, I would look in the mirror while dressed up and dolled up with makeup and hair done and think, "wow I feel pretty, but ugh if I didn't have these bags under my eyes." or, "ugh if my thighs weren't so thick, and I hate these hips." Other days and mornings before getting in the shower or getting dressed, I would look in the mirror and just completely tear myself apart and pick at all the parts of me that I hated. My cellulite, love handles, my long ugly toes, my wide hips and my thighs, my rolls, the list goes on. I was so mean to my body. No matter how much I worked out, and treated myself to self care it didn't matter, because what I was giving my body and my mind was hate and toxic energy. No wonder my body couldn't respond well to me. I was feeding it energy that never allowed it to thrive. No matter how hard I worked out and or how hard I restricted my food, my body didn't stand a chance at ever being good enough for me. The reason why is because of the emotional eating, and lack of self compassion and true self love. This victim mindset I took on would only let me be in a state of mind where my body could only give me back what I was giving her. And what I was giving her was a very toxic and defeated energy. When I started the mindset work and stopped hating my body, and began to feed my body the love it needed... things shifted. I started with my thoughts and words.

Today, I have a healthy relationship with the girl in the mirror looking back at me. I love her and tell her she is beautiful, sexy, and wonderful. I energize her with uplifting words and I never leave the mirror without saying at least one uplifting empowering compliment about myself. That energy now creates a healthy environment where I don't emotionally eat or shame myself for when I eat something that isn't considered healthy. I enjoy working out and feeding my body supplements and food that are good for me because it's how I love myself. The actions I do now are rooted in self love and not self loathing. If you deprive yourself, or if you create an "I don't care" mentality, then what you get back is the same from your body and environment. You should care, and above all, you should be happy. It's all in your mindset. Today I encourage you to start a new relationship with the mirror, if your past relationship with it was not in alignment with true self love.

Daily Journal Prompt:

1. What are some ways that you can feed your body love so that you can create an environment for your body to thrive and respond back the way you want to look and feel?

Affirmation: I am worthy. I am complete. I am valuable. I am loved. I am powerful. I am strong. I am a super conqueror.

DAY 36: SHOW UP FOR YOU

What does it mean to show up for yourself? For me it means being super clear on who you are and what you want and desire for your life, so that you can prioritize the actions and steps that will lead you to creating those things. And this, my dear, always starts by showing up for yourself first. We are always communicating to the universe what is important and the universe will reflect back to us exactly what we are communicating. And if your needs and desires are not being communicated as a high level of importance, then you will always find that your needs and desires are not being met. Showing up for yourself means making choices that set you up as a priority, worthy of receiving the best. Some actions that align with showing up for yourself are, creating a system in which you schedule the actions and activities that get you closer to your goals and desires. For example, let's say those activities are a mix of self care and business goals. Well… showing up for yourself means scheduling out and time blocking those activities in your calendar, and committing to showing up for yourself. Scheduling it means it's important and essential for achieving your desired results. If you were a sales person and you scheduled appointments to meet with clients, you would never ever even consider not showing up for that client. Even in the event of an emergency, you would still reschedule the appointment and show up. Well, it is the same for us. If we can not show up for ourselves, then eventually, we do not take ourselves seriously and our lives give us back exactly what we are communicating. So, if you are communicating you are not a priority and there's no need to show up for yourself, then you will find more lack and void in your life rather than finding more fulfillment.

Daily Journal Prompt:

1. How can you show up for yourself more often?
2. What will you put in place so that you become a priority?

Affirmation: I am worthy. I am complete. I am valuable. I am loved. I am powerful. I am strong. I am a super conqueror.

DAY 37: EMBRACE ALL THE EMOTIONS

If you have never seen Disney's movie "Inside Out," I highly recommend it. Although it's an animated movie made for children, it has so many lessons that adults can learn from. To quickly summarize the movie, you experience an 11 year old girl's life through all the emotions living in her mind. The characters are Joy, Fear, Anger, Sadness, and Disgust. These emotions help her navigate through life. But what we truly find rooted in the main lesson and takeaway is that happiness is not only about having one emotion all the time. Happiness is not only about feeling joy every moment of your life. We learn that there is some much more to life than just constantly feeling positive and joyful every moment of the day. In the movie we see that in a particular scene Riley, the 11 year old, achieves a deeper level of happiness when sadness takes control and overrides Joy during that moment. You also see moments where Riley feels fear and anger to help her decide and make choices. In conclusion it's important to note that it is totally ok and healthy to embrace all your emotions. There is nothing wrong with feeling emotions of sadness, fear, anger, and so on. Life is not about avoiding those emotions, but more about handling them in a healthy way. We can learn to embrace all the seasons of life with every emotion they bring. Our capacity to deal with our thoughts and emotions isn't a constant battle, but learning from them and navigating them with a healthy and sound mind. And again, remember, it's ok to feel all of it, even failure and disappointment. There's nothing wrong with you.

Daily Journal Prompt:

1. What emotions do you embrace?
2. What emotions do you not embrace?
3. How can you allow yourself to embrace all the emotions you feel moving forward?

Affirmation: I am worthy. I am complete. I am valuable. I am loved. I am powerful. I am strong. I am a super conqueror.

DAY 38: IT'S AN INSIDE JOB

Happiness, contentment, love, and abundance are never ever going to be found externally. The biggest mistake we make as humans is when we attach our happiness to something, or someone. The biggest lesson in life in truly creating joy and happiness is realizing that you have everything it takes inside of you already. You are whole and complete, and you can feel joy and love already from within yourself. It is not when something happens, or when someone comes into your life, or when you have something materialistic, or when you have the job, the promotion, or the money. You can be happy now because you have it already. It's inside of you. The only destination you need to run to is inside of yourself. Inside of your mind, your heart, your body, your source of life, your creator. It's getting to listen to your true voice, and feel the magic you are connected to. Going inside enables you to feel, to think, and to find clarity in the quiet and stillness, and not in the noise of the world. When you go inside you get to heal and nourish yourself and give yourself exactly what you need. Nothing outside of you can do that for you. Once you do the inside job, your expectations and desires start to shift. Your choices and decisions will be guided, and you have more clarity. When you are happy from within you align with doing more of what fulfills you and brings you more joy. You then cease to want and do things to make you happy, rather, you do them because you are already happy, and because they add to your happiness. For example you don't exercise to try and make yourself feel better. You exercise because you are happy and you care about your body, so you exercise because you want to be good to your body. Slowly you will see that your actions and behaviors are a reflection of the self love you have from inside. This will then show up in the relationships you have, and how you allow people to treat you. When you know your worth you don't choose relationships that treat you badly, or you don't seek out relationships in order to make you feel worthy or good enough. When you exude love from within you are emanating love and you become attractive to others. If you are constantly running to someone or something rather than running inside, you will always be forever chasing something for your happiness. And, my dear... that happiness is already inside of you.

Daily Journal Prompt:

1. What are your favorite things about your personality?
2. What is unique about you?
3. What is something you can give yourself to feel loved?

Affirmation: I am worthy. I am complete. I am valuable. I am loved. I am powerful. I am strong. I am a super conqueror.

DAY 39: TRUST YOURSELF

Building a strong trust for yourself is going to fuel your relationship with yourself in a really mighty way. Trusting yourself is connected with showing up for yourself, and strengthening your confidence and self worth. All of these parts of you are essential to aligning with your desires and goals in life. In order to achieve your goals it's going to always start with loving yourself unconditionally to believe you are good enough and worthy enough of having the success you desire. Trusting yourself will require you to get rid of the negative self talk and thoughts about yourself, and any self-criticism you make of yourself. Pay attention to your inner voice and how you react when you make a mistake, or how you feel when you forget things, or cancel plans, or delay the project, or when you don't stick to a goal you set. The more you perpetuate a negative self talk and any self-criticism, the less power you have to attain the self trust you need. Build on your strengths, uncover more of what your strengths are, and attempt new things that are not in your wheelhouse, and allow yourself to do them without judgement or self criticism. Remember to bring Grace around with you because she will give you self compassion for when you don't do things perfectly. Break the habits of not wanting to try new things. Stop trying to keep busy all the time with distractions like social media, or streaming shows to avoid doing the inner work you really need to do to build your strengths. Never look at a mistake as a regret or failure. Rather, look at everything as an opportunity to make you stronger. Surrender to the freedom that says there are no bad choices, there are no bad feelings. Every choice you make is a step towards your end result, and feeling all emotions along the way serves a purpose. Do not fear or regret. Everything is working out. Remember that you have everything in you to create the life you want.

Daily Journal Prompt:

1. Do you find yourself doubting and not trusting yourself when making decisions?
2. Do you find yourself not taking action because you fear possibly failing or doing it wrong?

Affirmation: I am worthy. I am complete. I am valuable. I am loved. I am powerful. I am strong. I am a super conqueror.

DAY 40: SET THOSE BOUNDARIES

As we continue to unravel more about self love and all the parts that help strengthen this love for ourselves, we have to talk about boundaries. Boundaries are crucial to cultivating a healthy relationship to yourself and relationship with others. Creating boundaries is having awareness of your individual needs and wants, and honoring those needs. When we don't set these boundaries, we let others override our needs, and we find ourselves sacrificing our priorities and health so that others get what they need. Boundaries allow you to set very clear intentions for your life that align with your health mentally, physically, and spiritually. When you lack boundaries you allow others to control your feelings and needs. Unhealthy boundaries, or lack of boundaries can weaken your own sense of true identity and authenticity, leaving you feeling disempowered. Lack of emotional boundaries leaves you powerless and will keep you in a lack and fear mindset. Most people who do not create emotional boundaries are fearful of losing friends, or being judged, and take on the responsibility of others' needs and happiness over theirs. Not having boundaries leaves you believing that your identity is rooted in external things and statuses. For example, " I am nobody if I am not in a relationship." "I am not important unless my children or partners are happy." Setting boundaries says that you are important and that you take responsibility for your happiness, your behaviors, your feelings, and your choices. Good boundaries are signs of emotional health and self respect. As we learned earlier, we are communicating to the universe how we want to be treated and what we feel deserving of. Setting good boundaries will align you with more pleasant experiences and relationships. It's ok to say no. It's ok to do more things you enjoy. It's ok to speak up when you are being mistreated or taken advantage of. It's important to protect your time, ask for help, and put yourself first. When you love yourself, you will set boundaries, because you will ultimately realize that setting boundaries attracts opportunities and people who love, respect, and appreciate your energy. It all starts with how you feel about yourself. If you feel worthy, valuable, and deserving of having the best life, then you will communicate exactly what you want to attract. It all starts with those boundaries.

Daily Journal Prompt:

1. Have you created strong boundaries for your life?
2. What are some boundaries you can put in place that create more peace for you?

Affirmation: I am worthy. I am complete. I am valuable. I am loved. I am powerful. I am strong. I am a super conqueror.

DAY 41: YOU ARE LOVED

You are loved, deeply, truly, and purely. Not because of anything you have done or accomplished, but because your creator loves you madly. The Bible says in Isaiah 54:10 'Though the mountains be shaken and the hills be removed, yet my unfailing love for you will not be shaken nor my covenant of peace be removed, says the Lord, who has compassion on you.' This beautiful verse sets a great reminder that God's kindness and love will never depart from us. He loves us and he has our best interest at heart. I truly believe that the desires and dreams we have in our hearts were placed by God. He wants us to attain those very desires. But we must remember that seeking things that are external to who we are and who were truly created to be will have us chase all the wrong things. We will create confusion, chaos, pain, and a lot of unnecessary havoc in our lives. When we forget the promises of God and we seek for love and validation and happiness outside of ourselves and our creator... our source of love, we will always end up empty. True fulfilment comes from within because it's where God lives. God is our peace. Philippians 4:7 says "And the peace of God, which passes all understanding, will guard your hearts and minds in Christ Jesus." When we choose to be in alignment with the same compassion, grace, forgiveness, and discipline that God reminds us of in His words, we will exude that love, and we will receive love and favor in our lives.

Daily Journal Prompt:

1. What are some ways that you can be more present to knowing and believing that you are loved?
2. What promises of God allow you to feel more loved and secure?

Affirmation: I am worthy. I am complete. I am valuable. I am loved. I am powerful. I am strong. I am a super conqueror.

DAY 42: TRUE LOVE

Today we end our self love revelation. My hope and prayer for you is that you have stepped into a relationship of true love for yourself. I pray that you have a clear realization that true self love is not about an emotion or an attraction. True love for yourself is not about a desire to be accepted or seen as special by others. Self love is not rooted in lack, scarcity, or fear, but is rooted in abundance and gratitude. True love allows you to draw closer to your truest essence and to your creator. True love seeks out internal growth and gives to you what you need in order to successfully enjoy life. True love allows you to experience life as a gift and receive all the blessings and experiences of life with confidence and self worth, because all of life seeks to grow you. True self love will allow you to walk as an agent of growth for others, because you have allowed growth in your life and are rooted in love, and therefore can give love abundantly. Love brings healing and joy. Love is the most powerful transformative energy that we can access.

Daily Journal Prompt:

1. What does your self love journey look like now?
2. What will your self love journey become?

Affirmation: I am worthy. I am complete. I am valuable. I am loved. I am powerful. I am strong. I am a super conqueror.

Part 3: Manifest

DAY 43: PLAN TO PROSPER

You have made it to your last 21 days. Congratulations! In these last 21 days, we are creating powerful affirmations and prayers that will align with your new self. It's the NEW YOU! We will continue to break down any walls and limitations that may be lingering, and step into a new possibility by speaking truths and words over our lives that reaffirm our new belief. Now we can heal from our past, because we have revealed and unravelled the layers of beliefs and false identities that were buried in our subconscious mind. Today you have more conscious awareness of the thoughts that consumed you and are aware of the emotional energies that may have disempowered you. Stepping into a new space with new found energy and a mind fueled in gratitude and love will empower you to continue healing and creating a new life different from the past. Reach your goals with no limits. Understand now that anything is possible and that God has an amazing plan for your life. God's word in Jeremiah 29:11 says "For I know the plans I have for you, declares the Lord, plans to prosper you and not to harm you, plans to give you hope and a future." Cling to these truths and promises over the next 21 days and let them encourage you, uplift you, and bring forth amazing transformations over your life.

Daily Journal Prompt:

1. What is the NEW YOU creating today for your future self?

Affirmation: Abundance is all around me. I have opportunities all around me to succeed. Success flows to me naturally. I am safe to follow my passion and my desires. I am grateful for all the success in my life. I am enjoying all the success in my life that shows up in different ways.

DAY 44: WHAT YOU WANT, WANTS YOU

I truly believe that when we get super clear about our desires, God will always orchestrate those very desires to be manifested in our lives. We don't have desires for things that are out of alignment with our purpose in life and the calling we were created for. Your soul's purpose that God placed in your very heart and spirit will be brought forth in its perfect timing. You may have to prepare by learning and developing yourself, but the truth is that you will reap the very desires in which you step into each day. Take delight in the Lord and he will give you the desires of your heart. Aligning with your calling and truest desire starts with clarity. Taking time to really ask yourself "What do I really want?" "How do I want to feel?" and "Why do I want that?" These questions are super important to get clear on before creating your next 21 day strategies to manifest your desired goals. What we find out most of the time when we look deeper into our desires or present goals, is that sometimes our goals are imposed by society or by popular opinions. Ask yourself what happiness looks like for me and what does that mean for me. Answering these questions will help guide you closer to having more clarity on your desires so that each day you can step into creating and aligning your thoughts and energy with that goal.

Daily Journal Prompt:

1. What do you want?
2. How do you want to feel?
3. Why do I want that?
4. What does happiness look like for you?

Affirmation: Abundance is all around me. I have opportunities all around me to succeed. Success flows to me naturally. I am safe to follow my passion and my desires. I am grateful for all the success in my life. I am enjoying all the success in my life that shows up in different ways.

DAY 45: EGO: EVERY ONE'S GOT ONE

Getting clarity of what your true soul desire is means getting your ego in check and knowing when a desire is your ego or your soul speaking. Some ways to know if it's your ego is by asking yourself these questions: "Is this desire more about pleasing others to get what I want?" "Does this goal energize me, inspire me, and make me feel true joy?" The ego's desires are normally things that have to come to you and not through you. Keep spending time quietly going within yourself to do the inside job. Doing the inner work will always lead you to find your personal rhythm and you will hear God's voice guiding you. Remember that our goal is to be in alignment with your authentic self... not with an idea of who we think we need to be, or what we should have based on what society tells us. When we are inauthentic, our ego will root itself in desires that build a persona for the world. Your ego fears not having and then is fueled by fear instead of abundance. Remember that the opposite of love and gratitude is scarcity and lack. Your ego will always push you to have more, do more, and want more. Your ego will also breed anxiety, and will always lead you to burnout vs being in alignment.

Daily Journal Prompt:

1. What goals or desires might you have that may be ego driven?
2. What, if anything is not working in your life?
3. How often do you feel burned out?
4. What brings you fulfillment?

Affirmation: Abundance is all around me. I have opportunities all around me to succeed. Success flows to me naturally. I am safe to follow my passion and my desires. I am grateful for all the success in my life. I am enjoying all the success in my life that shows up in different ways.

DAY 46: REJECTION IS PROTECTION

We are programmed to have very unhealthy thoughts about failure and rejection. These thoughts, as we know, will create emotional energies that leave us feeling discouraged and disempowered. When we associate rejection as a direct reflection of our self worth and inability to reach our desires, we hinder ourselves from opening ourselves up to new opportunities. This view of rejection will lead only to pain and constant upsets. But if you can understand that rejection is always a form of protection, then you will not spiral downwards to a place of lack and powerlessness. Rejection and failure are always there to teach and show us, and it's also revealing. Failed opportunities become opportunities to learn and grow and best of all guide us. This will give you the freedom to continue on your journey knowing there are so many wonderful and better things God is creating for you. Remember that what you want wants you back. You might not get the job you wanted, but the better job is out there for you, you might not be with the person you loved but soon you will be with the person you were meant to be with. Rejection never means you are not good enough, or worthy enough, but it means that you are better than the person or the opportunity that rejected you. Lastly, don't fall victim to instant gratification. What is designed and meant for you is coming for you. Don't settle for what is not meant for you. Instead, keep preparing patiently for that amazing blessing God is magically orchestrating for you.

Daily Journal Prompt:

1. How has rejection and failure felt for you in the past?
2. What are some rejections you have experienced in the past that you realize today were a form of protection?

Affirmation: Abundance is all around me. I have opportunities all around me to succeed. Success flows to me naturally. I am safe to follow my passion and my desires. I am grateful for all the success in my life. I am enjoying all the success in my life that shows up in different ways.

DAY 47: THINK BIG

God didn't give us small desires. He gave us desires bigger than ourselves. Things that make us uncomfortable and the things that seem impossible to us are those magical abundant gifts and blessings God has in store for us. Our human minds can't see the possibility of some of our desires actually ever coming true, but God does things outside of our thinking and understanding. The desires placed in our hearts are meant to challenge us and will require faith. He is ready to do big and mighty things in you and through you. If you find yourself wanting to settle or stay in the comfort zone, listen to your heart and you will hear it tugging at you to seek out that desire. It will never sit still, it will keep calling you. Whatever that goal or desire is, if it seems scary and unreachable then that is a great sign. Remember that the only limits you have were set by you and you only. And lastly, don't forget to do the inside work and get clarity of your goals. Let the ego go and sit with your creator and let Him speak to your soul.

Daily Journal Prompt:

1. What is your heart's desire?
2. Do you feel there are limits to your desires?

Affirmation: Abundance is all around me. I have opportunities all around me to succeed. Success flows to me naturally. I am safe to follow my passion and my desires. I am grateful for all the success in my life. I am enjoying all the success in my life that shows up in different ways.

DAY 48: NO SPIRIT OF FEAR

"For God has not given us a spirit of fear, but of power and of love and of sound mind." (2 Timothy 1:7). Fear is one emotion we must have a healthy relationship with. Fear will paralyze us, and it will lie to us. I love this acrostic that reminds us what we are saying when we let fear take control over our emotions and thoughts.

False
Evidence
Appearing
Real

Fear keeps your thoughts on the circumstances that could go wrong and it shifts you from abundance and gratitude to scarcity and lack. Functioning in a fear mindset says that things are fixed in the worst case scenario and tells you that there is nothing good that can prosper in the circumstances you are facing. But as the word of God says we were not given a spirit of fear. We were equipped with power and love and a sound mind to set our thoughts and our minds on truth and to find the evidence of possibilities and opportunities that are available for us. Don't let fear keep you paralyzed, ineffective, and rob you of the power you have to keep taking actions towards your goals. Understand that fear is a very normal emotion to feel, but embracing it and not letting it control you is the goal. Understand why the fear is showing up, and see what its purpose is at that present moment and what it may be revealing to you about what you are experiencing. Don't ignore the fear, but write about it, state it, and face it. When bringing this fear into the light it will shrink rather than grow. Lastly, look for inspiration and evidence around you that shows how this fear can be overcome. Looking for this evidence will shift you into a positive and optimistic attitude and emotion that moves you into a better state of emotional energy. You will be empowered to overcome the fear rather than fall into hopelessness.

Daily Journal Prompt:

1. How often do you find yourself struggling with fearful thoughts?
2. How can you embrace some of the fears you are present to?
3. Starting today, what fears will you let go of?

Affirmation: Abundance is all around me. I have opportunities all around me to succeed. Success flows to me naturally. I am safe to follow my passion and my desires. I am grateful for all the success in my life. I am enjoying all the success in my life that shows up in different ways.

DAY 49: YOU GOTTA HAVE FAITH

Faith is going to be an essential requirement in your journey towards achieving your goals and stepping into your calling in life. Along with setting your fears and doubts aside, manifesting healing, love, your dream career, and all other abundant opportunities, will require you to exude a tremendous level of unwavering faith. Your sole role in your life's journey is to step into your calling and show up everyday in alignment and belief that your desires are on their way. You are choosing faith over fear. Choose faith even when things do not seem to be working out, even when you fail at something, even when the rejection hits. It's all part of your journey. All things will work out. Faith is the power you will have to go deep down within yourself and know that things are working out just as they should, because they always do. Faith will empower you to keep taking the next steps even when you can't see where the next 10 steps will lead. Remember that you have faith in many things, just like driving a car, or flying on a plane. You can and will have faith in this journey, too. People have moved mountains with their level of faith, and so can you. If you find it hard to step into faith because you are worried or you feel anxious, then take time everyday to be aware that the energy that is fueling you is an energy of lack and scarcity. Your thoughts are creating an emotional energy that fears, rather than surrenders in gratitude and love. When you become present to that, you can practice a simple meditation in which you go inside and remind yourself and observe all of the ways you are abundant, secure, loved, supported, and how you already have access to freedom. This meditation allows you to give yourself the very thing you may be looking for externally. Or... start by journaling and ask yourself the following questions:

Daily Journal Prompt:

1. Where is there evidence in my life of love, freedom, security, and faith?
2. What do I look for externally that I can give to myself?
3. What are the possibilities available to me that I can control?
4. Name a time in which something that seemed scary worked out in the end?

Affirmation: Abundance is all around me. I have opportunities all around me to succeed. Success flows to me naturally. I am safe to follow my passion and my desires. I am grateful for all the success in my life. I am enjoying all the success in my life that shows up in different ways.

DAY 50: PATIENCE

In Ecclesiastes 3:1-8 we are reminded that there is a time and season for everything. God has made everything beautiful in its time. It's super easy to get frustrated and impatient when we are working towards our goals. We are programmed for instant gratification and we expect results immediately. Today we live in what I like to call a microwave society. Just like quickly cooking or heating up a meal in the microwave, this microwave society mindset has us wanting everything right now. Our technology can quickly connect us across the world and give us access to information with just a press of a button. No wonder we expect the same from everything else. Today, we expect everything in our life to be available on demand, but this lack of patience will quickly interfere with manifesting your goals and desires. Patience is a super power and it will be such a powerful tool in keeping you in alignment with truly creating the life you were meant to have, and not the life that you settled for. It will also protect you from making wrong decisions and choosing the options that were not meant for you. Patience allows you to accept that things are being orchestrated for you just the way they need to be... perfectly in its timing. This super power will strengthen you more and more each time you apply it in your life. It slows your temper, and anger, and rage, and will quickly put your ego in check. Patience allows you to be slow to react to your circumstances, and instead, will guide you in responding with self control. Lastly, practicing and being a conqueror of patience will bring forth the very things that are worth your time.

Daily Journal Prompt:

1. What are some things you are currently having a hard time having patience for?

2. What does being patient mean for you?
3. Does your lack of patience sometimes correlate to you trying to be in control of situations, events, or people?
4. What can you let go of in order to become patient, surrender, and be at peace?

Affirmation: Abundance is all around me. I have opportunities all around me to succeed. Success flows to me naturally. I am safe to follow my passion and my desires. I am grateful for all the success in my life. I am enjoying all the success in my life that shows up in different ways.

DAY 51: BE ABOUT IT

"Don't talk about it, be about it." - Bob Burns. If we could summarize the answer to the question "How can I manifest my goals and desires?" in just one quote it would be this very quote. You see, words and actions are just one small aspect of manifesting. If your actions and words are not in alignment with your inner being and belief, then nothing will truly change or manifest. Like the saying goes, "actions speak louder than words." Your words mean nothing when your actions are completely opposite of what you are saying. But even deeper than that, your actions mean nothing if your core being doesn't believe in what you are doing. For example, you can religiously go to church, and the act of going to church could seem to others that you believe in the practice of attending church. But if who you are everyday does not align with the belief of attending church, then no transformation ever occurs. If what you do doesn't truly mean anything and is not in response to who you are inside, then you will find yourself getting results in life that are completely opposite of what you wanted to create. Let's say your goal is to be a speaker, then you need to practice and do what a speaker does. You would need to embody the speaker you want to be today. What does the speaker do, practice, create, have, and so on? A speaker has their core messages and speeches always ready, learns how to deliver a message impactfully, has a way for people to find their speaker profile, and practices their speaking as often as possible. These actions are exactly in alignment with being a speaker, and the actions you would need to take each day. In other words, you are preparing and making a way for this role to manifest. So, just like this speaker example, we can apply the other goals and desires in our lives the very same way.

Daily Journal Prompt:

1. What does your future self do?
2. What are the ways of being you can be today that steps into that future version of yourself?
3. What new rituals and routines will you begin today?

Affirmation: Abundance is all around me. I have opportunities all around me to succeed. Success flows to me naturally. I am safe to follow my passion and my desires. I am grateful for all the success in my life. I am enjoying all the success in my life that shows up in different ways.

DAY 52: WORK BACKWARDS

One of the best strategies you can do to help create your intentions and strategies that align with achieving your goals is to work backwards. Starting from the future possibility and then mapping out exactly how you got to that finish line. Let's use the example of becoming a speaker who speaks at events and has a thriving speaking career. You will write out in detail what your day to day as a successful speaker looks like. What types of events do you speak at? Do you have a main event you personally host? Do you speak at international events? How do people find you and connect with you as a speaker? What messages do you speak about? What are you known for? What does your work space or creative space look like? How often do you speak at events? Who do you share the stage with? What type of people attend your speaking events? How are your events marketed and announced? Do you have collaborations and partnerships? The more you write out the details of how this speaking career looks and what your day to day activities are, the clearer it will be for you to create your map to achieving this goal. Once you have written down exactly what your future goal and career look like, you then start the process of mapping how you got to this place, and as we learned from yesterday, you now get to be about it. Each component of your future has a starting line. But in order for you to know what to start with you have to work backwards. And what is super amazing in practicing this method is that you get to pull from your future into the present moment, rather than pulling from your past into the present moment, which only creates more of the past. Working backwards also allows you to create intentions that will align with your end goal. So let's say that you wrote that you host events and share the stage with other speakers. The starting line to this may be that you networked and met other speakers who were looking for collaborations. Maybe you wrote that you met these speakers through networking events or online social groups. If that was part of your map then today you can start getting into those networking groups and social groups and building connections. If you said that your speaking messages were on a specific topic or modality, then today you could be mastering that topic and creating content that allows you to effectively deliver that presentation. And just like this example, you will take your personal future story and the parts of your story that are designed for your success, and you'll create explanations on how those specific parts manifested. Eventually you will have an entire map and strategy clearly aligning with the steps to get to your goals.

Daily Journal Prompt:

1. Today, begin to write out a letter to someone describing what you have accomplished exactly one year from now? Make sure to mention the goals you have achieved and describe the details of how you are spending your time. Add any other details about your life that you want to presently manifest.
2. Now that you have this letter, you can map out the action steps you took to create those possibilities. And as we learned on day 51, you can start being about it.

Affirmation: Abundance is all around me. I have opportunities all around me to succeed. Success flows to me naturally. I am safe to follow my passion and my desires. I am grateful for all the success in my life. I am enjoying all the success in my life that shows up in different ways.

DAY 53: VISUALIZE IT

Now that we have spent the last few days getting super clear on what you want and desire, our next steps in the manifestation process will require a good amount of time visualizing and feeling exactly what it will look like once you have achieved your goal. This aligns with our strategy of pulling from your future and bringing it into the present moment. Spend time everyday visualizing that you already have what you desire as if it's happening right now. Feel the abundance and ownership versus the lack and scarcity of not having it. Visualizing your end results as if it's happening now allows you to resonate with your future and sets your emotional energy to be in that alignment. Each day that you are "being" about your future self is a step closer to achieving your goals. Remember that your thoughts are either empowering you or disempowering you. You cannot create from a place of lack. So if most of your days are spent looking for your goal, becoming impatient, feeling anxious, or worried that your goal is not going to come into fruition, then that exact thought and energy keeps creating more of the past and more of the lack. But when you visualize your future as if it's happening right this moment, then you embrace a new mindset filled with thoughts of gratitude, excitement, and joy, which instantly creates a higher energy source that will empower you. Visualization is simply the act of daydreaming. You can practice visualization in many ways. Some ways to do this are by creating some daily rituals and intentions to practice visualization as much as you can throughout the day. You could visualize the first thing in the morning, right before bed, during meditation, while driving, while taking a bath or shower, and any other time of the day you choose. The more you visualize, the more you are activating your subconscious mind to go to work for you. It will program your brain and body to be familiar with that new future. And lastly, it will build your motivation and empower you to reach that goal.

Daily Journal Prompt:

1. What are the feelings and energy you feel when visualizing the goals you will achieve?
2. Set intentional times and commit yourself to visualizing your future. Feel those energies as much as possible through the day.

Affirmation: Abundance is all around me. I have opportunities all around me to succeed. Success flows to me naturally. I am safe to follow my passion and my desires. I am grateful for all the success in my life. I am enjoying all the success in my life that shows up in different ways.

DAY 54: YOU REAP WHAT YOU SOW

We have all heard the saying, "You reap what you sow." And for me, this quote could not be more important when it comes to manifesting your desires and goals. Simply put, you will get back what you put in and what you invest in. I also believe that what you sow abundantly will come back exponentially. We have the power to create so much in our life by just the way we serve, give, and what we allow to serve us. How we invest our time and energies is a direct communication with our universe of what we want and accept. Reaping and sowing are essentially about what will be available to us as blessings, or as lessons and consequences. When we are constantly getting the things we do not want in life, then it's a time to reflect and do the inner work, and see where you may not be in alignment with what you truly want to manifest and reap. Many times we will find that we are allowing things in our life that are opening the wrong doors and are not growing or serving us. What we entertain with our minds can be feeding the very things we don't want in our lives, but we may be naive or ignorant to what those things could be. Taking responsibility for your life and for the results you are getting in life is hard for most people to do. Most people want to blame something or someone, or say that their circumstances were out of their control. But the reality is, we have a lot more control of what happens to us than we think. Now... I am not saying that there is nothing in this world you don't have control over. We know we can not control people, world disasters, or as 2020 showed us, we can't control pandemics and economic crashes, but we can control how we respond to those situations. I believe that our responses and actions in those times is ultimately how we create the life we want. Yes... there are some things out of our control, but our mental and spiritual health, our physical health, our personal economic situations, our personal relationships, and the opportunities that come to us are within our control. So think about the ways in which you invest your time and energy. What do you sow everyday in your mind, in your health, your friendships, your community, your marriage, and so on. What you feed is what grows, and again… what you sow you will reap.

Daily Journal Prompt:

1. What energies, actions, thoughts, emotions, and forms of entertainment are you present to that you are sowing on a regular basis?
2. What new energies, opportunities, and feelings would you like to reap more of?

Affirmation: Abundance is all around me. I have opportunities all around me to succeed. Success flows to me naturally. I am safe to follow my passion and my desires. I am grateful for all the success in my life. I am enjoying all the success in my life that shows up in different ways.

DAY 55: LETS MANIFEST

Everyday we are either creating more of what we want or more of what we don't want. And this all starts with our energy. Remember that your thoughts create emotional energy, and where our focus goes energy goes. When you are in the highest state of emotional energy you are in your prime state of mind to manifest. As we learned on day 10 it is important for you to become aware of where you fall on the emotional vibration scale. Self awareness of where you are on this scale will help you navigate your focus. Our emotions will form our choices, actions, and the way we choose to show up. Our thoughts create our reality. The bible says, "As a man thinketh in his heart so is he." God gave us an amazing gift within our human mind. Our ability to learn and think and choose is what gives us favor as humans. Your thoughts become reflections of who you really are. Even when you say something or think a thought that is not in alignment with what you really believe, the energy and vibration of your way of being will not produce the results you intend to produce with those thoughts and words. This is where practice and faith must step in to transform you from the inside out. You will know a tree by its fruit. And just like a tree, what we produce in our lives will reflect what beliefs we are rooted in. What waters your way of being? What is fueling your actions and choice?

Daily Journal Prompt:

1. How do you want to feel most of the time?
2. Why do you want to have those feelings?

Affirmation: Abundance is all around me. I have opportunities all around me to succeed. Success flows to me naturally. I am safe to follow my passion and my desires. I am grateful for all the success in my life. I am enjoying all the success in my life that shows up in different ways.

DAY 56: REBOUND

As we learned yesterday, our thoughts create our reality, because the emotional energy that is created when having those thoughts ultimately guides our choices and our thoughts. If you are thinking thoughts on the emotional vibration scale such as anger, fear, jealousy, hate, or boredom, then you are creating from a very low energy source. These thoughts are creating lack and scarcity, and disempower you to take actions towards your goals. Now... as a reminder from day 37, it is ok to have feelings that are not always positive or fall high on the scale. Embracing all our emotions is healthy and it is very important to root yourself in love, self compassion, and grace. But, today we are going to talk about getting good at the rebound. Mastering the rebound will be a key part of aligning yourself to manifesting your goals. Just like our daily rituals, whatever thoughts we have the most of have become what we are experts in. And, although it is ok to feel those lower emotional feelings sometimes, it's not ok to stay there. We want to learn how to rebound. Just like in sports, this rebound technique creates a better athlete who will go out on the court and increase his or her chances of winning the game with their team. If you read about techniques to perfect the rebound in sports, it's all about making a conscious choice and having the right mentality, being the first to react and follow through to pursue the ball. And, just like that, we can learn to master the rebound when it comes to our thoughts and emotional energies, consciously choosing to rebound and reset with a higher emotion such as gratitude. Remember, it takes a conscious effort to defeat the subconscious battle. Learning how to rebound allows you to choose wisely and prioritizes your well being and commitment to creating a life that you deserve and desire.

Daily Journal Prompt:

1. What are your current struggles that may be pulling your thoughts and energy down vs up?
2. What can you choose today to be grateful for that can rebound your thoughts and energy back into being a priority in your own life?

Affirmation: Abundance is all around me. I have opportunities all around me to succeed. Success flows to me naturally. I am safe to follow my passion and my desires. I am grateful for all the success in my life. I am enjoying all the success in my life that shows up in different ways.

DAY 57: REPROGRAM

Our subconscious mind is the deep part of us that takes in 40 million bits of information every second. After a filtering process in our brain we only perceive 5 to 9 bits per second. These 5-9 bits per second is what becomes our perception of reality. Our subconscious mind is what controls all our automatic processes like tying our shoes, driving home from work, riding a bike, walking, and playing an instrument. Even our unhealthy habits all reside in our subconscious mind. All our habitual reactions and thought patterns come from our subconscious. What we think about the most comes from our subconscious mind. Having this knowledge is very important, because if we can align our subconscious mind to what we want to create in our life, then we will have more success in achieving goals and creating more of what we desire. Revealing to yourself what has been rooted deeply in your subconscious, as we did on your first 21 days, is step 1 in reprogramming those beliefs and ideas that are in conflict. Partnering with your creator to co-create with him the very desires he has placed in our hearts starts with accepting the truths and promises of God over your life, and deeply rooting them into your subconscious mind, so that your actions and spirit will be in alignment with the very truths of God. Practicing your affirmations and meditating on those truths daily will have you focus your energy and thoughts to those new beliefs. Once your focus and energy goes there, you will see more and more evidence of those truths. This process over time begins to slowly take over your old beliefs and patterns.

Daily Journal Prompt:

1. What are you choosing today to attract into your life?
2. What new beliefs will you reprogram into your subconscious mind to align with what you are choosing to attract?

Affirmation: Abundance is all around me. I have opportunities all around me to succeed. Success flows to me naturally. I am safe to follow my passion and my desires. I am grateful for all the success in my life. I am enjoying all the success in my life that shows up in different ways.

DAY 58: WHAT YOU RESIST... PERSISTS

You can't solve the problem with the same thinking that created the problem. If you're complaining about what you don't want, you will only create more of what you don't want. "Why can't I get it right?" "Why can't anyone understand me?" "Why can't I get what I want?" "Why do things always go wrong?" "Why can't I stop eating badly?" "I can't seem to lose weight." "I will never be organized." "My kids never listen to me." Do these sound familiar? Whenever our thoughts are focused on what is not working vs. what is working, we lose fuel and energy to create more of what we want. We fall back into a lack and scarcity mindset vs. a mindset of abundance. And remember, we cannot create from lack. Achieving goals means setting our eyes on our goals and visualizing the end result before it arrives. If we are constantly resisting the things we don't want, we will fall deeper into the present struggle. To use a simple example, when you go to a restaurant, you don't tell a server what you don't want on the menu, right? You tell the server what you want. And in life, it's the same. We are constantly communicating what we want more of, and if our thoughts and energies are always focused on what is going wrong and what we are trying to run away from, then we spiral into that web of constant struggle. Rather, we can begin to communicate and focus on what we want and what we are running towards. Our reticular activator will go to work and give us more evidence of the things we focus on. Remember to embrace all your feelings, rebound, and refocus. Lastly, cut out the elements in your life that are not feeding and helping you create more of what you do want. Relationships, food, ect.

Daily Journal Prompt:

1. How much time do you feel you spend resisting or focusing on what you don't want in life?
2. Do you find yourself focusing on what you don't have and what is not working vs. what you do have and what is working?
3. What will you choose today to be your focus?

Affirmation: Abundance is all around me. I have opportunities all around me to succeed. Success flows to me naturally. I am safe to follow my passion and my desires. I am grateful for all the success in my life. I am enjoying all the success in my life that shows up in different ways.

DAY 59: CLARITY IS KEY

To elaborate more on day 58 we realize that most people are inclined to focus on what they don't want, which is a problem. When setting goals it's important to be specific. It is super important to write down your goals. Writing down your goals will increase your chance of achieving it by 70%.

Also, be clear on why you want these goals? Write down what achieving these goals ultimately provides for you. For example, if you write down a goal to achieve a certain level of promotion in your career or maybe to reach a salary goal (like making over six figures a year), write down what achieving this goal provides for you that is important to you? Get deeper in understanding why achieving this goal is essential for your happiness. How may this goal enhance your quality of life?

Lastly, unravel the desires of these goals a little more and write down how you may be able to attain the result through other means. For example, if you wrote down that making over six figures gives you security, peace, or success, then how might you be able to feel secure, peaceful, or successful in other ways? Or better yet, where in your present life do you already feel secure, peaceful, and successful?

Daily Journal Prompt:

1. What are your health goals?
2. What are your relationship goals?
3. What are your personal and spiritual goals?
4. What are your financial and career goals?
5. Write down your why for each of these goals.
6. Read your goals daily.

Affirmation: Abundance is all around me. I have opportunities all around me to succeed. Success flows to me naturally. I am safe to follow my passion and my desires. I am grateful for all the success in my life. I am enjoying all the success in my life that shows up in different ways.

DAY 60: BE INTENTIONAL

Now that you have clarity on your goals and desires, living with intention to be in alignment with these goals, values, and passions will be an essential part in manifesting these goals. One of the best things I started to do was create daily intentions to keep me focused on the actions needed to achieve my goals. This became part of my morning routine. Setting daily intentions gave me the ability to create choices and habits throughout the day that would align me with strategies I needed to achieve more of what I wanted in my life. Once you are super clear on the things you desire more of in your life, living intentionally will create more of those things. Intentions develop healthier habits and responsibility to keep you connected to yourself and resonate with your truth. Developing a habit of creating daily intentions will enhance your life in so many ways, because you are creating a life that is filled with purpose and a life that says you are worthy, you are important, and you are dedicated. Lastly, living intentionally means that you take control of your day vs. the day taking control of you. One of the ways I love to write out intentions is to describe how I want to feel rather than the things I need to do. What ends up happening is my actions for the day will bring me exactly what I wanted to feel for the day. Here is an example of how I would write down a daily intention during my morning journaling session.

"Today will be creative, abundant, exciting, uplifting, and energetic. Today opportunities will flow, and people will be inspired, touched, and moved. Today I will see great organization, communication, and inspiration."

Now that I have written these intentions down, I will create a day in which I will seek these very things. For example, I wrote, "today will be creative and abundant." In this case, in order for me to be creative, I will prioritize actions in doing creative work. I may work on creating content such as a video, or graphics for my business, or write marketing content for social media. I also wrote that opportunities will flow. In this case, I will seek out evidence in which I could connect with and grab on to opportunities. I also wrote that people will be inspired. I may again create content that will inspire someone, or maybe I'll send an intentional uplifting message to someone and build healthy relationships.

All of these intentions are in alignment with my personal, spiritual, relationship, health and financial goals.

Action step: Write out 3 to 4 intentions for how you want your day to feel and turn out. Practice writing out daily intentions that align with your goals and desires every morning, until it becomes a daily habit as easy as writing out a to do list for the day.

Affirmation: Abundance is all around me. I have opportunities all around me to succeed. Success flows to me naturally. I am safe to follow my passion and my desires. I am grateful for all the success in my life. I am enjoying all the success in my life that shows up in different ways.

DAY 61: ATTACHMENT VS COMMITMENT

One of the best ways to stay joyful and grounded in faith is to detach yourself from the specificities of how exactly your goals will come to fruition. The most important part is to stay committed to the vision and results you are seeking. You will practice the art of surrendering most days. You may not know exactly how things will work out, but having the faith and surrendering the details will make your journey a lot more pleasant. Believe that God's spirit will guide you and all you have to do is show up and be in alignment with your intentions. The more you practice this level of surrendering, the more you will see that each step you are taking is guided and prompted to lead you to exactly where you need to be. When you get too consumed and attached to your own plan, or set on the ways you think it should go, how it should be done, who needs to be there, where it should be, and so on, then you will miss out on the opportunity to see how God is perfectly orchestrating your ultimate success. Now... this does not mean you should not have a plan. You definitely should have a plan, but it means surrendering the details on the how, and having unwavering faith that your plans will be guided perfectly. This means that if part of your plans seem to be changing or not going the way you thought it should go, don't get frustrated or give up. Instead, surrender to knowing that God has something else in mind and it's still a perfect plan. Be open to having your requests show up differently than you had thought they would show up. When you are open to all the possible ways your desires may show up, your journey becomes a lot more free, and enjoyable. Commit yourself completely to your calling and your desire, and live full out to achieve it. Trust that it is yours to claim.

Daily Journal Prompt:

1. Has there ever been a time in which you experienced a blessing or opportunity that you had sought out to achieve, but the way in which you received it was not how you thought it would happen? Maybe how you met someone, or how some unexpected money came, or a random connection led you to a bigger, more fruitful one?

2. How present are you to the parts of your goals you may be attached to vs. committed to?

Affirmation: Abundance is all around me. I have opportunities all around me to succeed. Success flows to me naturally. I am safe to follow my passion and my desires. I am grateful for all the success in my life. I am enjoying all the success in my life that shows up in different ways.

DAY 62: MANIFEST WITH GRATITUDE

The best place to be when working towards your goals is to be in gratitude every step of the way. When you are in a place of gratitude you will have more peace and less stress. Gratitude shifts your perspective and your focus, and allows you to see everyday, every hour, every moment as an opportunity. When you shift to an attitude of gratitude, you take advantage of all the parts of you and the resources around you. You give thanks for your sound mind, your body, and its ability to move and create. You give thanks for the resources you have available to you. Maybe it's your house, your car, your computer, your phone, your friends, your neighbors, and so on. When your focus is always seeing the opportunities and abundance that you have access to, you align with more abundance, more opportunities, more resources, and you find the solutions you need. Gratitude is giving thanks even for the things unseen. It aligns with the belief and faith that they are available to you and headed to you. As we learned yesterday, surrendering and staying committed to your goals will keep you from a place of frustration and worry, and it moves you to a place of gratitude and confidence. The more you give thanks and the more you celebrate, the more joy you create. The opposite of gratitude is to complain and focus on what is lacking and not available to you. Complaining and constant worrying is a sure way to create a life that is harder, full of struggle, void of real joy, and a whole lot of stress. You can not manifest from a place of such lack. Complaining is the complete opposite of gratitude. If you find yourself complaining more often than showing gratitude, you will always find and attract reasons to complain, and you will have no reasons to celebrate. So... it's simple. Find more reasons to celebrate and give thanks, and watch how gratitude expands and you attract more things to be grateful for.

Daily Journal Prompt:

1. What are you currently grateful for that you will celebrate?
2. What actions will you take on today to create the future you want?
3. What will you do today that will be beneficial to your growth?
4. What are you excited to manifest in your life?

Celebrate each thought, each step, each action, each level of growth that brings you closer to your goals and desires.

Affirmation: Abundance is all around me. I have opportunities all around me to succeed. Success flows to me naturally. I am safe to follow my passion and my desires. I am grateful for all the success in my life. I am enjoying all the success in my life that shows up in different ways.

DAY 63: DESIRE VS BELIEF

As we complete your 63 day journey, I want to take us back to our first 21 days. As we learned during our first 21 days, Neuroscience has shown that most of our decisions, actions, emotions and behaviors come from the programming in our subconscious mind. And, our core beliefs that shape our lives all stem from our subconscious. So… you can desire to have a better job, more money, a successful business, and find a perfect mate, but your life will always be a reflection of the programs and beliefs in your subconscious mind. This is why it will be critical to question and reveal what your beliefs are about your self worth, money, love, people, God, and so on. If your deeply rooted beliefs are in conflict with what you are consciously working on achieving, then be aware that this is where self sabotage begins. The conflict of your desires vs. beliefs is where resistance enters, and beyond that, it is why you will miss the opportunities that are right in front of you. Your mind wants to keep you safe and only looks for the evidence to keep you exactly where you have programmed yourself to be. Your subconscious mind is always looking for evidence to validate your beliefs of worthiness or lack of worthiness and where you have deemed yourself to belong. It will keep you responding to how you have programmed yourself to be. Having this awareness is essential so that you become more present to the thoughts and patterns which are always a reflection of what you believe. Your beliefs therefore, must be stronger and more powerful than your desire to succeed. You must believe that you are worthy of success and that success is yours to achieve. A daily practice of mastering your thoughts and meditating on God's truth and promises will begin the process of transforming your desires into your truth and new belief.

Daily Journal Prompt:

1. What subconscious beliefs might you be present to that are in conflict with your desires?
2. What evidence can you find that contradicts your limiting beliefs?
3. What will be the new possibilities and truths you will create moving forward?

Affirmation: Abundance is all around me. I have opportunities all around me to succeed. Success flows to me naturally. I am safe to follow my passion and my desires. I am grateful for all the success in my life. I am enjoying all the success in my life that shows up in different ways.

FINAL THOUGHTS

Congratulations! You have made it through a super transformational 63 day journey that is created to help you step into alignment with your goals and desires. I pray that during these past 63 days you have created a deeper level of awareness and can now truly step into a new and incredible future. I pray that you have experienced transformation and growth in your mental, physical, and spiritual health. My desire for you is that you live a life fueled in love and gratitude, and that you stand firm on the truths and promises of God. After these 63 days, I pray that you walk into your future with confidence and unwavering belief and faith that all of your desires and dreams are yours to have and you are worthy of receiving them. Let go of the memories of the past and old identities and beliefs that do not serve you. Today you are stepping into your future with abundant love and power, and you are celebrating all the abundance and love that is on its way to you. Thank you for allowing me to play a role in your transformation. My heart is bursting with love and gratitude for each and every soul whose life has been touched, moved, and inspired in any way by this book. I would love to stay connected with you, and if you would love more resources and guides to master your mindset visit www.victoriadume.com for more information.

With Love and Gratitude,
Victoria Dume

AFFIRMATIONS

I am worthy. I am complete. I am valuable. I am loved. I am powerful. I am strong. I am a super conqueror. I attract success. Abundance is all around me. I have infinite potential. I am deserving. I have opportunities all around me to succeed. Success flows to me naturally. I am connected to my creator and I am guided. I am safe to follow my passion and my desires. I know my purpose and I am walking in my purpose. I am grateful for all my success in life.

I am enjoying all the success in my life that show up in different forms. I give abundantly because abundance is all around. I am courageous. I go after the things I want. I am a positive thinker. I am a magnet for success. I love to take action on my ideas. I am always inspired to take action. I see abundance all around and I am abundant. I am a daughter of the most high and He provides for me always. I lack nothing. I am whole and complete. I create value for those around me. I encourage myself everyday. I think optimistically. I give myself and others compassion. I am successful in all areas of my life. I am passionate about my life. I can control my emotions. I know that my happiness is a choice and I choose happiness.

I let go of the beliefs of success and abundance that have been governed by others. I allow myself to let go of beliefs that were never mine. I accept myself for who I am, with all the experiences I have had. I am ready to step into my true potential. Everyday I align with truth, love, healing, and abundance. Everyday I express gratitude for my blessings and opportunities. I receive with gratitude. I choose to see evidence of God's love and goodness all around. I shine my light because I am free. Opportunities and success come to me in unexpected ways. I leap and take actions with unwavering faith. I am in discernment to the choices I need to make because my spirit is led by my creator. I am joy. I am love. I am proud to follow my desires and go after what I want with confidence. I have a unique path. I am equipped with the tools I need to succeed. I am grateful for the support that is available to me. I surrender the need to control and I surrender the need to know how all things will work out. I believe that all things always work out as long as I am in alignment with God's love, truth, and promises.

I give love because I am loved. All my needs are met. I lack nothing. I love seeing my goals come to fruition. I am always inspired to express my thoughts and ideas. I am creative and I always express my creativity. I use my creativity to create value for others. I desire to be a vessel and source of transformation for those around me. I always receive with a heart of gratitude. I am deserving of the love and success and abundance available to me. I am healthy, safe, joyful, and thriving. I am focused on being the best I can be. Everyday I am becoming more confident. My potential to succeed is limitless. I am in tune with my body and I respond to its healthy desires. My future is full of promise. I am proud of who I am becoming.

Made in the USA
Monee, IL
12 January 2022

88133744R10079